The Wesleyan Tradition

Wesleyan University Press

*Published by
University Press of New England
Hanover and London*

The Wesleyan Tradition

Four Decades of American Poetry

Michael Collier, editor

Wesleyan University Press
Published by University Press of New England, Hanover, NH 03755
© 1993 by Wesleyan University
All rights reserved
Printed in the United States of America   5   4   3   2   1
CIP data appear at the end of the book
A list of copyright holders appears on page 271.

Contents

Second Decade

Third Decade

Fourth Decade

Preface

From the beginning of this project I set out to compile an anthology that would be more than a mere survey of the Wesleyan University Press poetry program. I wanted the anthology to show how the Wesleyan program since 1959 helped to create fundamental changes not only in American poetry but also in the way poetry has been published. I felt this could be done best by fashioning an anthology that included the strongest and most representative work of the past four decades. From my initial reading of each of the approximately 250 Wesleyan volumes I made a large, inclusive anthology containing more than 1,200 poems. From this selection I made a series of successively smaller anthologies until I arrived at something resembling the present collection. Edward Hirsch, David St. John, and David Wojahn provided me with valuable readings of the manuscript and helped to correct some, but certainly not all, of my oversights. I am grateful for the help they have given me and hope the present version shows some of the fine and considered attention they gave the earlier one.

During the process of deciding what constituted the strongest and most representative work of the Wesleyan program, I found it necessary to establish a few criteria. As a result, I decided not to select work by the English poets Donald Davie, D. J. Enright, or Jon Silkin, even though they are poets whose work I admire greatly. The influence of English poetry on American Academic poetry during the forties and fifties was so pervasive that I felt their work made no specific comment. However, it is interesting to note that in Norman Holmes Pearson's 1969 anthology, *Decade: A Collection of Poems from the First Ten Years of The Wesleyan Poetry Program*, the selection of Davie poems is larger than all but that of James Wright and David Ignatow. I also left out many of the "protest" poems written by poets of the sixties and seventies. I included stronger and more subtle political poems that represented the sentiment of the "protest" poem without embracing its sentimentality. Because the page limit to which I agreed for the anthology restricted my use of long poems and poems in sections, I have also left out entirely and regrettably sections from the book-length poems of Julia Budenz and Mark Irwin, as well as longer poems of many other Wesleyan poets. Many Wesleyan poets made important and influential translations of poems from other languages and included these translations in their

Wesleyan books, and in the eighties the program had a translation series that published more than a dozen volumes. I regret not finding a place for some of these translations. Close readers of contemporary American poetry will notice that the anthology appropriates a number of poems not originally published by Wesleyan. These became "Wesleyan" poems when the Press published the selected or collected work of a poet who had not originally published with the program or who, having left the program, came back to publish a retrospective volume. Purists may see this as fudging the issue of the Wesleyan tradition, but I couldn't resist the opportunity to enlarge the tradition by including these poems. In general I have also tried to work against the notion of this anthology as a "Greatest Hits" volume and yet at times, no matter how popular or often anthologized a poem might have been, or how many times I imagined the anthology without it, I found myself committed to the poem because of its intrinsic and undeniable power.

I have organized the anthology by decades and have presented the poets in their order of appearance during that decade. I have also kept all the work of each poet together, in the decade of first appearance, regardless of how many books or across how many decades the poet published with Wesleyan. This method might create a slight amount of confusion if a reader looks for a poet in each of the decades where he or she published. For example, all of John Haines's work is found in the first decade, though he published Wesleyan books in the seventies and eighties as well. By doing this I hoped not to use the arbitrary divisions of the decades to "turn struggles of taste and values," as Paul Zweig has written, "into a marching order for textbooks," but rather to invite a reader to see all at once the length of a poet's relationship with Wesleyan as well as gain some insight into the development of the poet's work.

I offer an apology to all Wesleyan poets not included in the anthology. My hope is that *The Wesleyan Tradition* is only a starting point and will encourage readers to seek out the rest of us. For me the reading of so many books in a relatively short period was a humbling and powerful, if not exhausting, experience. The opportunity to edit this volume has been extremely gratifying, and the burden of the honor weighed on me throughout the process.

I want to thank Terry Cochran for suggesting this project and for inviting me to undertake it. Suzanna Tamminen at Wesleyan University Press has provided me with much help. Many friends and students, directly or indirectly, have helped through their ideas, encouragement, and patience. Jeannette Hopkins, Tom Sleigh, Ken Botnick, Garrett Hongo, Stanley Plumly, Howard Norman, Ira Sadoff, Beret Strong, and Ellen

Bryant Voigt, I am happily indebted to you. My deepest and most enduring thanks go to my wife, Katherine Branch.

New Haven   M. C.
April, 1993

Introduction

My first encounter with the Wesleyan Poetry program took place more than twenty years ago in Arizona at the main branch of the Phoenix Public Library. Books by James Dickey, James Wright, Louis Simpson, Robert Bly, David Ignatow, Philip Levine, and Donald Justice had already been well-used by the time I began taking them home, for two-week furloughs, in 1971. For a nineteen-year-old, with three semesters of college, who was trying to imagine a literary life for himself in the middle of what was just then being called the Sunbelt, I had no way of appreciating the significance of these books. The poems of Wright, Bly, Dickey, Levine, and Simpson were unlike anything I had ever read. Simpson's "American Poetry," with its "stomach that can digest / Rubber, coal, uranium, moons, poems" and its humorous "shark" that "contains a shoe" and utters "cries that are almost human," was typical of the forceful immediacy and urgency I felt when reading the early Wesleyan poets. It was an urgency that was carried beyond the first-decade poets and into the seventies, and could be heard in James Wright's "I am almost afraid to write down / This thing," which begins "The Old WPA Swimming Pool in Martins Ferry, Ohio." As a group what these poets seemed most "afraid" of was a vision of America they could not turn away from. This vision demanded, as James Dickey wrote, that we witness "not just the promise, not just the loss and the 'betrayal of the American ideal,' the Whitmanian ideal . . . but the whole 'complex fate,' the difficult and agonizing *meaning* of being an American, of living as an American at the time in which one chances to live" (Lazer, 75). "The whole 'complex fate'" and "agonizing meaning" was that penchant in the American character that could produce, as James Wright noted, "so many things . . . that begin nobly and end meanly" (4). If the form of these poems was unfamiliar to me—freer, more open than high-school textbook poetry though calmer and less inchoate than the Ginsberg and Ferlinghetti I had read—their description of America and of what it meant to be an American were not unfamiliar. In a pure and direct way these poets made it clear to me that the struggle to make sense of one's life through poetry is a struggle, on one level, with form.

These poets also demonstrated that poetry was connected to the larger cultural forces and changes taking place within American society. It spoke of dying cities, of the solitude and isolation of the suburbs, of the size of

the country, of the Vietnam War, of immigrants, of the middle and work-
ing classes, as it carried the "news" all Americans needed to hear about
their country. In the broadest sense many of the early Wesleyan poets
represented the democratization of poetry that was taking place through
the creative writing programs in American universities and colleges. Jus-
tice, Levine, Donald Petersen, and William Dickey, all early Wesleyan
poets, had been members of the same poetry-writing workshop at the
University of Iowa in the mid-fifties. The tie, though not a causal one,
between the Wesleyan poetry program and creative writing programs
would remain strong and influential throughout the decades. As a result
of this connection, the early Wesleyan books not only contained an aes-
thetic for beginning writers like myself, but they also proved that poetry
and the universities had an implicit institutional relationship and that
even while many early Wesleyan poets rebelled against the Academic
and institutionalized poetry of New Criticism, the rebellion was taking
place, so to speak, within the palace.

This is not to say that poets such as Bly, Wright, James Dickey, Simp-
son, and Levine did little to change the kind of poetry being written in
America. On the contrary, poetry and the writing of poetry had become
an activity of phenomenal proportions in the seventies, eighties, and
nineties because of the profound effect the early Wesleyan poets had on
the narrow dominant aesthetic of the fifties. The history of these
changes, the history of this phenomenon, can be seen in the Wesleyan
poetry program. No other university or commercial press poetry list can
provide as wide a view or as broad a history of contemporary American
poetry as can the Wesleyan list, and in this way *The Wesleyan Tradition:
Four Decades of American Poetry* stands as a definitive record of Amer-
ican poetry written since the late fifties.

Providing a record or survey of such a distinguished tradition carries
an obvious significance, but as a reader of this anthology I would be im-
patient if a record or survey were the limit of the anthology's accom-
plishment. The central role occupied by the Wesleyan poetry program
during the last four decades of American poetry offers a unique oppor-
tunity to assess not only the poetry program but also contemporary
American poetry since 1959. Furthermore, as an assessment the an-
thology implicitly places the tradition of Wesleyan poetry within the
broader changes taking place in American culture, so that a reader can
see not only what kinds of poems are representative of the Wesleyan
poetry program but also gain an understanding of why such poems were
written.

When I first discovered the Wesleyan Poets, in 1971, the program had
already exceeded its first decade. An anthology entitled *Decade: A Col-*

lection of Poetry from the First Ten Years of The Wesleyan Poetry Program, edited by Norman Holmes Pearson, had been published in 1969. In his introduction to the anthology, Pearson remarked that at the start of the program, in the late fifties, "Somehow the publishing of poetry, though not the writing of it, had been in the doldrums. The Wesleyan series helped to stir the air." The immediate model for the program came from the Yale University Press Yale Series of Younger Poets, which since 1919 had been publishing first books of poems by poets under the age of forty. Except for Yale poets Muriel Rukeyser, Paul Engle, James Agee, William Meredith, and Eve Merriam, the Yale Series, in thirty years, had done little to distinguish itself, until W. H. Auden became its editor in 1950. Auden's decade of editorship yielded Adrienne Rich, W. S. Merwin (twice), John Ashbery, James Wright, John Hollander, and William Dickey. Auden demonstrated that the institutional support of a university press combined with a strong editorial vision could produce a distinguished poetry list. All of Auden's choices, except perhaps Ashbery, were committed to writing exemplary and distinctive Academic poetry in which technique, surface, literary allusion, artifice, and compression were highly valued. This style, a product of late-Modern, New Critical attitudes, prized distance and control, objectivity and irony as poetry's highest achievements. Academic poetry flourished, as Robert Von Hallberg has pointed out, in the "decade after the war" when there had been "a demand in America for those signs of cultural coherence that help to ratify [the] imperium" (28). The cultural coherence of the Academic poets came not so much from American culture as it did from the English tradition of lyric poetry, filtered through the New Criticism of John Crowe Ransom, Allen Tate, Ivor Winters, and Robert Penn Warren. In the late forties and fifties the Academic style had been given a lively embodiment through the work of Richard Wilbur. Acknowledging the pervasiveness of Wilbur's influence, Randall Jarrell once noted, in an address to the Library of Congress on the state of American poetry, "and then there is another larger group of poets who, so to speak, came out from under Richard Wilbur's overcoat."

Richard Wilbur was teaching at Wesleyan University at the time Willard Lockwood formed Wesleyan University Press in 1958. Lockwood, as the first director of the Press, and Wilbur, as an advisor, decided to commit part of the energy of the new press to publishing contemporary poetry. As outlined on the dust-jacket copy of early books, "The purpose of The Wesleyan Poetry Program is to publish regularly collections of outstanding contemporary poetry in English. Manuscripts are welcomed from anyone. They are read by the distinguished poets and critics who comprise the especial editorial board that makes publishing recommendations. There are no restrictions on form or of style. The Program attempts, quite simply, to publish the best poetry written today. Its single criterion of acceptance is excellence."

Donald Hall, William Meredith, and Norman Holmes Pearson were the members of the first poetry editorial board. The original intention of the program was to bring out, simultaneously, hardback and paperback editions of four books each year. The first four poets represented were Barbara Howes, Hyam Plutzik, Louis Simpson, and James Wright. The books met with critical success and the new publishing venture was praised as a model for future university press poetry programs. In the decades that followed, the number of books the program published annually varied, from as few as four to as many as sixteen, and the editorial board rotated its membership.

In the aftermath of Wesleyan's success approximately fifteen university press poetry series were established. Along with the Wesleyan program these have filled a gap left in the publication of poetry by the indifference of the commercial presses. In his preface to *Vital Signs: Contemporary American Poetry from the University Presses*, Ronald Wallace quotes David Wojahn on the importance of the university press poetry series: "Nearly thirty years after Wesleyan started its poetry series, poetry has been more defined and shaped by the university press than by the commercial or small house" (29). Although many of the early Wesleyan poets had published first books before coming to the program, the majority of poets published by Wesleyan were first-book poets. The history of the Wesleyan University Press poetry program demonstrates that Wesleyan was often a starting place for poets who, once their reputations were made, moved on to commercial houses. This springboard aspect is an inherent feature of many university press poetry programs. Recently, however, Wesleyan has welcomed back a number of its early authors, James Dickey, David Ignatow, and Harvey Shapiro, as well as provided a place for mid-career poets such as Gregory Orr, Heather McHugh, Rachel Hadas, Sherod Santos, and Donald Revell. In the almost thirty-five years since Wesleyan began filling the publishing "gap" of poetry, that gap has become the most real and significant territory for mainstream American poetry.

Although many university presses followed Wesleyan's lead as a publisher of poetry, Wesleyan's method of selecting its manuscripts remained distinctive. Most university press poetry programs have relied on a single editor or an individual guest judge to make editorial recommendations. Wesleyan's "especial editorial board" of poets and critics helped keep the Wesleyan program alive to the widest possibilities of the newest work being written.

The method at times made it possible for individual board members to lobby hard for special interests without having to take responsibility for the long-term features of the program. Consensus as an editorial policy also led to some regrettable decisions. Wesleyan had published Philip Levine's very successful first full-length collection, *Not This Pig*, but when he submitted *They Feed They Lion*, the board turned it down, twice. In the Press's file on the decision, the brief comments by the board record that two of the readers were largely in favor of Levine's manuscript, but that the third member, who strongly opposed it, was able to sway the other two.

On the surface the incident involving Levine's *They Feed They Lion* might appear to be the result of an editorial decision reached through consensus, but it also signalled the aesthetic limits the program would rarely venture beyond. Levine's *Not This Pig* is emotionally direct and unrelenting in its indictment of capitalist America; nevertheless, it has manners, rhyme and meter; it behaves itself. But *They Feed They Lion*, though it uses rhetoric skillfully (the title poem could not be more highly cadenced and controlled), also projects the scary anarchy that broke through the surface of the "imperium" of mannered America during the era of inner-city race riots and anti-war demonstrations of the sixties. *They Feed They Lion* represented what the establishment poets of the fifties could be said to have feared most, disintegration of the cultural fabric of American life and disavowal of the modes of poetic discourse they had labored to justify. The decision not to publish Levine's second book is typical of the decisions that throughout its history has kept the Wesleyan program solidly within the mainstream and normative in contemporary American poetry. But in light of these limits, it is important to underscore that the early Wesleyan board, especially in Wilbur, Meredith, Hall, Pearson, and Hollander, showed generosity and foresight in understanding aesthetics antagonistic to their own. The ability of the early board members to identify the best poets of a rebellious generation allowed the Wesleyan poetry program to take advantage of larger and more far-reaching changes taking place within American culture. This ability, more than anything else, is what established the program's reputation.

The creation of the Wesleyan program profited from this period of vigor and confidence in America's poetry. This confidence came from a common sense of purpose at the center of American culture, a sense of purpose buoyed by the post-war boom and expansion, regardless of the ominous shadows cast by McCarthyism and the Korean "conflict." Robert Von Hallberg writes that American poets of the fifties were confident of being in "the honorable tradition of addressing the audience that felt greatest responsibility for the refinement of taste and the preservation of a national culture" (34). The fact that the mainstream culture was so well defined and, in Von Hallberg's words, "effective at dominating cultural institutions" (35) provided the resistance that gave rise to an avant-garde. Although the early Wesleyan poets were hardly members of the fifties avant-garde (the Beats and Black Mountaineers), their poetry was stubbornly committed to finding new forms of expression. Both the Beats and the early Wesleyan poets had taken up Walt Whitman's democratic ideas about poetry. Although each group would exploit different aspects of the great poet for their own, their interest in Whitman revealed a common desire to reinvent American poetry.

At the same time that changes were taking place in mainstream American poetry, the institutions that had supported this poetry were changing as well. The system of American land-grant universities was expanding rapidly. Graduate creative writing programs on the model of the Iowa Writers' Workshop proliferated. The English departments, which had given homes to professor poets such as Ransom, Tate, Blackmur, Winters, and Warren, were now host to poet professors who took the New Critical approaches of the previous generation and adapted them to their creative writing workshops. By looking at the evolving connection between universities, poets, and publishing, it is easy to surmise that a program such as Wesleyan's arrived to meet the future publishing needs of university creative writing programs.

From a larger cultural perspective what was happening in contemporary American poery began to resemble Tocqueville's description of the literary arts in a democratic society. In *Democracy in America* Tocqueville wrote: "Taken as a whole literature in democratic ages can never represent, as it does in the periods of aristocracy, an aspect of order, regularity, science, and art; its form will, on the contrary, ordinarily be slighted, sometimes despised. Style will frequently be fantastic, incorrect, overburdened, and loose—almost always vehement and bold. Authors will aim at rapidity of execution, more than at perfection of detail . . . The object of authors will be to astonish rather than to please, and to stir the passions more than to stir the taste." Tocqueville was responding to, and in fact lamenting, the expansion of the cultural center in democratic ages—art and poetry, the aesthetic taste, emerging from individuals and constituencies as consensus rather than from cathedrals and courts. For poetry in particular this widening cultural center meant that the traditional geographical hubs for poetry, such as New York, Boston, and, since the Second World War, San Francisco, would expand to include colleges and universities located in places like Iowa City, Fresno, St. Paul, Ann Arbor, and Black Mountain.

From within the circle of establishment and Academic poets, the widening of the American cultural center was not yet so apparent. In his acceptance speech for the National Book Award in 1960, Robert Lowell described the two major camps in American poetry as "raw" and "cooked." This simplified matters, and took the important differences between the poets represented in Donald Allen's *The New American Poetry* (1960) and Donald Hall, Robert Pack, and Louis Simpson's *New Poets of England and America* (1957) at face value. It also had the effect of reducing aesthetic distinctions to matters of table manners and cultural nutrition and ignored the deeper changes that had taken place. The confidence that allowed establishment poets of the fifties, including Lowell, to see themselves as upholders of a universal American literary taste began to crumble, however, as the institutional structures of publishing and education shifted and broadened their bases. But perhaps the larger reason for the breakdown in confidence was that American culture as a whole had begun to question the domestic and foreign policies of its government. The pressures that the Beat and Black Mountain poets had put on the Academic poets throughout the fifties was no longer coming from the periphery of the culture but radiated from the center as well. The Wesleyan poetry program took advantage of the changes occurring in mainstream American poetry by establishing a publishing enterprise suited to the democratization of art and culture that had begun in the fifties and would continue to accelerate over the next three decades.

The Sixties

In his 1963 essay "A Wrong Turning in American Poetry" Robert Bly wrote, "Our recent poetry is [also] a poetry in which the poem is considered to be a construction independent of the poet. It is imagined that when the poet says 'I' in a poem he does not mean himself, but rather some other person—'the poet'—a dramatic hero. The poem is conceived as a clock which one sets going. This idea encourages the poet to construct automated and flawless machines. Such poems have thousands of intricately moving parts, dozens of iambic belts and pulleys, precision trippers that rhyme at the right moment, lights flashing alternately red and green, steam valves that whistle like birds." Bly's attack on American poetry is aimed both at the Academic verse of the period—with its emphasis on conventions, manner, and decorum instead of feeling, spontaneity, and sincerity—as well as at the Black Mountain poets who by focusing so heavily on William Carlos Williams had fostered, in Bly's words, an "American isolationism" born of the "Americanism of material, words, meter, and attitude as subjects for poetry" (*The Fifties*,

2:13). Both kinds of poetry had devalued the "image," which Bly believed was Modernism's most significant achievement. Bly wanted poetry to return to the early roots of Modernism and to the energy and innovation of the generation of 1917 which had found its most expressive and important homes in European and Latin American poetry. Besides his concern for the image, Bly criticized American poetry for its nineteenth-century obsession with "technique." "When poets talk of technique," Bly wrote in his well-known essay "Looking for Dragon Smoke," "they are usually headed for Jail." In general, Bly, Wright, Simpson, Dickey, and Ignatow believed that imagery grew out of the spontaneous and associative activities of the imagination which would give them unguarded access to the world of the unconscious. The image was the key to unlocking the door of the psyche, both collective and individual, behind which lay the truth of one's experience. Bly's method, which dominated American poetry for more than a decade, was supposed to release the image "from imprisonment among objects." Such a release, Bly wrote at the end of "A Wrong Turning in American Poetry," would have the curative effect of freeing American culture from its "technical obsession" and of reversing the dark processes "of business mentality, of human effort dissipated among objects, of expansion, of a destructive motion outward."

Bly provided the most passionate critical voice for a school that became known as Deep Imagism. If at times Bly's criticism was hectoring and contradictory, it was unequivocal about the direction in which mainstream American poetry was headed, away from the enervated verse of the Academy with its reticence and manners, good sense and equilibrium, stricture and restraint, toward an open, more inclusive, democratic, and associative poetry that produced what critics later called the "emotive imagination." Although "A Wrong Turning in American Poetry" was published in 1963, it described changes that had begun to take place in American poetry during the fifties.

Bly's claim for the "image" was large, but it was not the only new claim for poetry being made in America. Charles Olson published his essay on "Projective Verse" in 1950. Ginsberg had given his first public reading of "Howl" in 1954. John Ashbery's *Some Trees* appeared in 1956. Frank O'Hara's mock manifesto "Personism" and Robert Lowell's *Life Studies* were both published in 1959.

Perhaps the most important group that arose in the fifties was the Confessional poets. Robert Lowell, Sylvia Plath, W. D. Snodgrass, John Berryman, and Anne Sexton had been schooled in Academic verse and throughout their careers retained an allegiance to formal poetry. But the Confessional poets used convention and form as scaffolding on which to hang the seemingly unvarnished facts of the poet's often dramatic and tragic life. In Confessional poetry the distance between the poet and the poem disappeared. Autobiography replaced history. For the early Wesleyan poets, the Confessional mode represented a way in which to speak with sincerity and honesty about what mattered most.

The Confessional poets also had the important effect of being models of passionate if not reckless living for younger poets. Philip Levine has provided an example of such a model in a memoir about John Berryman as a teacher at the Iowa Writers' Workshop in 1954. "These were among the darkest days of the Cold War," Levine writes, "and yet John was able to convince us—merely because he believed it so deeply—that nothing could be more important for us, for the nation, for humankind, than our becoming the finest poets we could become" (541). This unswerving personal commitment to poetry, to one's art, became an important part of the atmosphere of creative writing workshops where the vocabulary for discussing poetry began to include more expressive or emotive terms, so that young poets were encouraged to "take risks," or insure their poems had "earned the right" to say what they were saying.

Whereas Deep Image poetry freed poets to explore the unseen and invisible, to confront the convolutions of the psyche, Confessional poetry, either by directly using the material of one's life or through personae, permitted poets to dramatize their personal experience. Early Wesleyan poets such as Simpson, James Dickey, Levine, Richard Howard, as well as James Wright and Bly to some extent, all became actors in their own poems. There was a freshness in writing such as Levine's "The Cemetery at Academy, California": "On a hot summer Sunday / I came here with my children / who wandered among headstones / kicking up dust clouds." Or in Dickey's "The Performance": "The last time I saw Donald Armstrong / He was staggering oddly off into the sun, / Going down, of the Philippine Islands."

But the history of the Wesleyan University Press poetry program's first decade is not only a history of innovation and revolution; it is also a history of the waning influence of those poets who, in Jarrell's phrase, had come out from under Wilbur's overcoat. Vassar Miller, Robert Bagg, Donald Petersen, W. R. Moses, David Ferry, and Barbara Howes all produced an interesting and distinctive poetry. In David Ferry's "My Parents en Route," for example, a haunting dream portrait of his parents "catafalqued" asleep in their beds is created by Ferry's consummate handling of formal devices. Donald Petersen, in "Ballad of Dead Yankees," gives life to an old convention through the boldness and near absurdity of the poem's subject:

> *Where's the swagger, where's the strut?*
> *Where's the style that was the hitter?*
> *Where's the pitcher's swanlike motion?*
> *What in God's name turned life bitter?*

Audaciousness and formal skill are also evident in what I like to think of as Alan Ansen's quirky and beautiful "vanishing" sestina, "A Fit of Something Against Something," which also satirizes the claims of free verse:

> *New rebels will not master*
> *Forms pointlessly austere.*
> *They feel they will be*
> *Screwed by that alien order,*
> *That Gestapo sestina,*
> *Cats, its the most ungone.*

The end of the first decade of the Wesleyan program marks the end of its period of greatest influence on American poetry. Wright, Bly, Levine, Justice, Dickey, Simpson, Ignatow, Howard, and Ashbery all left the Press for commercial publishers. The seventies and following decades of the program would be devoted primarily to publishing poets influenced by the work of the first-decade Wesleyan poets.

The Seventies

The end of a decade of experimentation and rebellion from within the mainstream of American poetry coincided with a general flattening of cultural energy in the country. A highly conventional Deep Image or surreal poem had emerged, as empty and predictable in its concerns as the Academic poem, which it replaced, had been in the fifties. By 1971 parodies of Deep Imagism such as Harvey Shapiro's friendly but pointed "Hello There!" began to appear, and an impatience from critics and poets concerning the opacity of Deep Imagism could be found in essays and reviews of contemporary poetry.

> *Hello There!*
> for Robert Bly
>
> *The poets of the midwest*
> *Are in their towns,*
> *Looking out across wheat, corn,*
> *Great acres of silos.*
> *Neruda waves to them*
> *From the other side of the field.*

> *They are all so happy*
> *They make images.*

Bly's influence wasn't limited to a kind of "happy," ham-fisted, poet-in-overalls, image-making, however. His magazine *The Fifties*, and then *The Sixties*, along with *kayak* and *Lillabulero* helped to establish and promote a serious and influential tradition of surrealism in contemporary American poetry. Outside the Wesleyan program Mark Strand, W. S. Merwin, Bill Knott, Charles Simic, and William Matthews had developed styles in the surrealist mode. Except perhaps for Matthews, these poets produced image-based poems quite different from the kind that Bly and Wright produced. In 1973 Paul Zweig, in an essay entitled "The New Surrealism," noted that Bly's Deep Imagism "is more concerned with spiritual exploration than with surreal language. His plea for 'imagery,' and against traditional rhetoric, brings him closer to Rilke, Vallejo, and Neruda, than to the provocations of Breton." This division between the spiritual side of Deep Imagism and the more intellectual and "shocking" side of a purer surrealism is played out among several Wesleyan poets of the seventies. Russell Edson, Michael Benedikt, and James Tate, with their absurd and mischievous sense of humor, their fractured fables for the imagination, and their emphasis on surface, are much closer to the linguistic attitudes of Breton. The Wesleyan poets most faithful to Bly's "spiritual exploration" are John Haines and Vern Rutsala. Rutsala in his prose poems and Haines in his short lyrics represent classical Deep Image concerns about the dark, mysterious regions and dreamscape of the unconscious.

The Wesleyan poet who found a way to bring both the spiritual and linguistic sides of surrealism together was Charles Wright. "The New Poem," published in his second Wesleyan book *Hard Freight* (1973), represents a kind of High Deep Imagism or High New Surrealism:

> *It will not resemble the sea.*
> *It will not have dirt on its thick hands.*
> *It will not be part of the weather.*
>
> *It will not reveal its name.*
> *It will not have dreams you can count on.*
> *It will not be photogenic.*
>
> *It will not attend our sorrow.*
> *It will not console our children.*
> *It will not be able to help us.*

During the seventies, as Charles Wright published four books with Wesleyan, he developed away from the high Deep Imagism of "The New

Poem" and its minimalist emotional scale. Yet he has remained a poet for whom the image, which he builds upon with a lavish and obsessive care, is still the most powerful and basic unit of poetic construction.

If the freshness and originality that had marked the innovations in American poetry during the sixties had become conventions by the seventies, so too had some of the features of university press poetry publishing. The concept of a poetry series had spread to commercial houses such as Houghton Mifflin and George Braziller and in the late seventies to Alfred A. Knopf. As a result the Wesleyan poetry program found itself in competition not only with other university presses but with commercial houses as well. The poetry lists at Atheneum and Farrar, Straus, & Giroux had expanded in the sixties and boasted some of the best recognized and original poets. This competition made it more difficult for Wesleyan to attract or keep, perhaps even to identify, the best poets of the next generation. While the seventies at Wesleyan produced many fine and distinguished poets, the overall profile of the decade is primarily one of first-book poets, working deftly in the period style.

That a period style in surrealism and the Deep Image developed so rapidly in American poetry of the sixties is an indication not only of the need for a new direction in poetry but also of the influence of creative writing programs. Cataloging the diction of Deep Imagism in 1974 ("breath," "snow," "future," "blood," "silence," "eats," "water") Robert Pinsky noted, "somewhere, on some campus in America, a young poet is writing a sentence with all or nearly all of the totemic words" of surrealistic diction (165). At its most conventional and formulaic, this writing was made for the democracy of the classroom. It stubbornly resisted traditional prosody, was brief, and could be handled with the expressive critical vocabulary of the workshop. This style, which Pinsky dubbed "one-of-the-guys surrealism," possessed the migratory habits of American culture as well, and, in spite of Shapiro's "poets of the midwest," the surrealist diction was as comfortable in the city as on the farm, in Tucson as Ann Arbor.

But Pinsky discovered a relative health in the poetry of America and like Bly, though without Bly's proselytizing, called for a change in the kind of poem being written. Pinsky found surrealist and Deep Imagist poems limited because they trusted "perception . . . more . . . than reflection," and eschewed ideas because they were "obstacles" to discovering the "large, blank, irreducible phenomena" that were, to surrealists, the "truest incarnations of reality" (165). Pinsky asked that poets return to more expansive forms, to take up meditative and discursive modes, and to exploit the "prose virtues" of poetry.

Pinsky's reading of American poetry in the mid-seventies is particularly relevant to this anthology because he uses a number of Wesleyan poets to make his case concerning the possibilities of post-Deep Imagism and American surrealist poetry. For Pinsky, James Wright's "Two Poems about President Harding" is an exception to the surrealist rule of producing "blank, irreducible phenomenon." Wright's poem, according to Pinsky, reveals the "unsuspected, essential parts of the invisible web of thoughts covering the world" (166). The revelation of this web is something that Pinsky believes is usually dependent upon "a rather proselike, sensible context or frame" (166). As an example of a poem with a "sensible context or frame," Pinsky offers "The Soldier" by David Ferry. "The Soldier," with its clear, dramatic barracks scene, is characterized by Pinsky as attaining "a proselike openness of statement while incorporating and using a distinctly contemporary sense of the material world, its obdurate inhumanity and its human uses" (172). Ferry's poem, though quite different in its formal concerns from James Wright's poem, is a model of those qualities—restraint, clarity, and wholeness—that Wright himself pursued in his own work.

If we could combine the essence of Wright—what Pinsky describes as the "surrealist enterprise"—with Ferry's "proselike openness of statement," we would have a poem that points ahead to the dominant mode in American poetry from the late seventies until the present. That poem, a hybrid of sorts, was already being written by Simpson, Levine, and Dickey and would be taken up by seventies poets James Seay, Richard Tillinghast, Anne Stevenson, Clarence Major, and, to some extent, Ellen Bryant Voigt. Broadly speaking, this poem was a form of dramatic lyric that, depending on the poet, emphasized either the song-like quality of the lyric or the narrative movement and detail of story-drama. The immediate source of this dramatic lyric had come from the Academic poets and their precursors such as Ransom and Allen Tate. Although a lot of shifting and jostling had taken place in mainstream American poetry during the sixties, by the end of the seventies the center still found the qualities of control and reticence to be useful virtues. The lyricism that had been muffled by the intellectual and argumentative structures of the Academic style and had been declared conventional by many poets of the sixties began to return in poets such as Ellen Bryant Voigt. The opening stanza of Voigt's "Claiming Kin" is characteristic of the best and most rigorous of the new dramatic lyric:

> Insistent as a whistle, her voice up
> the stairs pried open the blanket's
> tight lid and piped me
> down to the pressure cooker's steam and rattle.
> In my mother's kitchen, the hot iron spit

> on signal, the vacuum cleaner whined
> and snuffled. Bright face
> and a snazzy apron, clicking her long spoons,
> how she commandeered the razzle-dazzle!

Perhaps what linked poets as diverse as James Wright and Ferry with those such as Ellen Bryant Voigt was the forceful presence of a governing tone or voice. In an essay published in the *American Poetry Review* in 1978, Stanley Plumly wrote, "tone seems to have displaced the image as a 'technique of discovery'" (24). The shift in emphasis from a poetry governed by traditional prosody or by the minimalism of surrealist diction resulted, Plumly believed, in "a free verse more flexible than ever . . . to accommodate a wider, more detailed, even contradictory range of emotional experience—yes, accommodate and control" (24). Plumly had discovered in the American poetry of the seventies that as tone had become more intimate, more evocative of the voice and personality of the poet, the "territory of the poem became more detailed, discrete, named" (24). To say that tone and voice are the most significant aspects of American poetry since the mid-seventies simplifies the complexity and diversity of work written in the past twenty years. It also has the effect of broadening the definitions of those words until they become nearly meaningless or at best fuzzily associated with, as Ira Sadoff has pointed out, "tone of voice," "mood," "point of view" and even "personality" (238). But it was not Plumly's intention to create a reductive description of mid-seventies American poetry; rather, tone and voice were ways to approach what Plumly saw as the increasingly formal characteristics of a ubiquitous free-verse "prose lyric" (27).

If Pinsky's ordering principle for American poetry in the mid-seventies was discursiveness—a wandering inside the materiality of the poem, in both its ideas and things—Plumly saw tone and voice as instruments that gave such wandering its control. Although Pinsky and Plumly recognized the power of the image as an icon or emblem, and the importance of the Modernist inheritance the image represented, they both criticized Deep Imagism and surrealism for producing poems that were too reductive. Plumly summed up the overall frustration with the period style in this way: "the image alone has no voice" (25).

The development of the dramatic lyric as a common mode from the seventies until the present was also helped by the influence of Confessional poetry. Confessional poetry created a kind of radical tradition of the self and offered an immediate and seemingly inexhaustible source of "voice"—the poet's own life. James Wright, whose own poetry reflects the development of the contemporary dramatic lyric, remarked in a 1978 interview that "my own life is the only thing I have to begin with. It seems to me an aesthetically legitimate as well as a morally legitimate thing to try to figure out what one's own life really is" (176). The positioning of the self in the poem, depending on how it was handled, allowed poets to recreate, no matter how personal and intimate, any state of mind or human predicament. It is not an exaggeration to say that the dominant mode of American poetry, as reflected in the majority of Wesleyan poets published since the late seventies, has been a discursive, personal narrative, written in free verse that is tightly controlled by tone and voice. Even poets who have continued working in traditional forms subsumed convention to the overall atmosphere of tone and voice. Although American poets for more than a decade had invested heavily in Deep Imagism and surrealism, the period style had written itself out and had left poets searching for ways, through their personal experience, to write about the "obdurate inhumanity and . . . human uses" of the material world.

The permission that Confessional poets granted young writers of the sixties and seventies was a permission to explore and create their own myths. These myths, though largely about the middle class and its suburban and mental landscapes, began to admit narrative shape and detail back into mainstream American poetry. The struggle by poets to define who they were not only as Americans but as individuals with unique voices was also part of the invitation implicit in the democratization of poetry by creative writing programs. This invitation became so powerful that, as Sadoff points out, "searching for a voice" is now a cliché of the creative writing workshops (238).

The Eighties and Nineties

As the Deep Image had done in the sixties and seventies, the prose lyric would come to dominate the poetry produced in creative writing workshops from the late seventies until the present. Unlike Deep Imagism, the terms of the "prose lyric" have always been broader. Wesleyan poets from the eighties working in this mode are as diverse as Garrett Hongo and Elizabeth Spires, Pattiann Rogers and Yusef Komunyakaa, Jordan Smith and Jane Hirshfield. The prose lyric possesses all the qualities of directness, sincerity, and honesty that had been the goal of many of the Wesleyan poets of the first decade. Garrett Hongo in "The Hongo Store" provides a powerful example of how the prose lyric produces a personal myth:

> *My parents felt those rumblings*
> *Coming deep from the earth's belly,*
> *Thudding like the bell of the Buddhist Church.*

> *Tremors in the ground swayed the bathinette*
> *Where I lay squalling in soapy water.*

And Elizabeth Spires in "Globe," with delicacy and exactitude, brings us back to one of her earliest memories:

> *I spread my game on the cracked linoleum floor:*
> *I had to play inside all day.*
> *The woman who kept me said so.*
> *She was middle-aged, drank tea in the middle of the day,*
> *her face the color of dust layered on a table.*

All prose lyrics have in common a surface realism of particular details which are used to establish a dramatic event in a specific time and place. The convention of time and place has created what Charles Altieri calls the "scenic" mode. Although the "scenic" mode characterizes many of the poets published by Wesleyan in the eighties and nineties, it is not the only period style represented.

Since the late seventies the poetry of John Ashbery has exerted a considerable influence on American poets. In part its evasions and ellipticisms, its iconography taken from popular culture, its playful use of cliché, its determination to subvert the old verities of love and beauty have provided an antidote to the "scenic" aspect of the prose lyric. As an antidote the Ashbery style has also been easily appropriated by creative writing workshops, resisting the emotive critical vocabulary of the workshop while allowing young poets to focus on the processes of language and to investigate the way in which consciousness and experience emerge through syntax. By the mid-eighties Ashbery had infiltrated mainstream American poetry enough to have established a signature mode in a younger generation of poets. Wesleyan poets Jane Miller, Olga Broumas, Ralph Angel, Bin Ramke, Donald Revell, and Brenda Hillman show the effect of Ashbery in their inventive work.

In the late seventies and early eighties, while the influence of the prose lyric and John Ashbery had established itself firmly in creative writing workshops, two movements—one reactionary and the other avant-garde—began developing on the fringes of mainstream American poetry. The reactionary movement has been loosely called New Formalism and is represented by poets and critics such as Dana Gioia, Brad Leithauser, and Joseph Epstein. The New Formalist aesthetic is characterized by a return to the conventions of the Academic poetry of the fifties. Brad Leithauser's essay "Metrical Illiteracy" criticized the tradition of American free verse for its formlessness, unmusicality, and self-involvement. The criticism in Leithauser's essay was mainly directed at those products of democracy, the poems written by poets trained in creative writing work-shops. Another New Formalist critic, Robert McPhillips, believed that a renewed attention to form would allow "a significant number of younger poets to think and communicate clearly about their sense of what is of most human value—love, beauty, mortality" (207).

Lamenting the loss of American cultural coherence and purpose last felt in the fifties, New Formalism paralleled the conservative turn that had taken place in America during the seventies and eighties. New For-malism had little influence on the Wesleyan poets of the eighties. Jordan Smith, Sherod Santos, and Judith Baumel write elegant and formal poems which occasionally employ traditional conventions, but on the whole they are more interested in creating an intimate and direct voice, typical of the prose lyric, and in this way they oppose the "robust little music box," which Leithauser argued for in "Metrical Illiteracy."

Whereas New Formalism attempted to regain some of the aesthetic ground taken from it by the creative writing workshop prose lyric, an avant-garde movement that identified itself as Language poetry devel-oped in opposition to everything that was not iconoclastic. Although in recent years, Language poetry, especially critical theory based on it, has become part of university creative writing and literature curricula, it has been primarily situated outside traditional cultural institutions. In fact Language poetry's main purpose is to criticize and deflate the coercive forces—political, social, and cultural—created by traditional institutions such as universities. As a result, Language poetry attempts to explore the ways in which traditional structures of language force poets to mis-represent the occasions of their experience. In many ways Language po-etry contains the passion and energy that was found in the early Deep Image rhetoric of Robert Bly, yet it is closer to the technique-driven aes-thetic of Olson's Projective Verse and therefore is suspicious of the pow-erful feeling and emotion Bly demanded that poetry embrace. The influence of Language poetry on the Wesleyan poets of the eighties and nineties has been very slight, and yet in the work of Susan Howe, Donald Revell, and Walid Bitar a reader encounters some of its concerns.

The Wesleyan Tradition is not meant to predict in any specific way the trends and movements that might arise in the next ten or twenty years in American poetry. Rather it offers a way in which to assess the Wesleyan University Press poetry program's original and on-going func-tion—to publish what in the broadest terms was truly the best in Amer-ican poetry. In doing this the program has helped to define and develop a poetry that is clearly American, one that is both popular and serious, that defines, criticizes, and supports the democratic institutions of American culture, and that in four decades has come to represent the cultural pluralism of democracy anticipated by Tocqueville more than one hundred and fifty years ago.

Works Cited

Altieri, Charles. *Self and Sensibility in Contemporary American Poetry*. Cambridge University Press, 1984.

Bly, Robert. "A Wrong Turning in American Poetry." Reprinted in *Claims for Poetry*, ed. Donald Hall. University of Michigan Press, 1984.

———. "Looking for Dragon Smoke." In *Naked Poetry*, ed. Stephen Berg and Robert Mezey. Bobbs Merrill, 1969.

———. "The Words of Robert Creeley." In *The Fifties*, vol. 2. 1959. Reprint by Hobart and William Smith College Press in association with *The Seneca Review*.

Dickey, James. "Louis Simpson." In *Babel to Byzantium*. Farrar, Straus and Giroux, 1968. (Also reprinted in *On Louis Simpson*, ed. Hank Lazer. University of Michigan Press, 1968.)

Epstein, Joseph. "Who Killed Poetry?" *Commentary* 86 (August 1988).

Gioia, Dana. *Can Poetry Matter?: Essays on Poetry and American Culture*. Graywolf Press, 1992.

Leithauser, Brad. "Metrical Illiteracy." *New Criterion*, vol. 1, no. 5 (1983).

Levine, Philip. "Mine Own John Berryman." *Gettysburg Review*, vol. 4, no. 4 (Autumn 1991).

McPhillips, Robert. "What's New about New Formalism." In *Expansive Poetry*. Storyline Press, 1989.

Pearson, Norman Holmes. *Decade: A Collection of Poetry from the First Ten Years of the Wesleyan Poetry Program*. Wesleyan University Press, 1969.

Pinsky, Robert. *The Situation of Poetry*. Princeton University Press, 1976.

Plumly, Stanley. "Chapter and Verse." *American Poetry Review*, vol. 7 (January–February 1978).

Sadoff, Ira. "Hearing Voices: The Fiction of Poetic Voice." In *An Ira Sadoff Reader: Selected Prose and Poetry*. University Press of New England, 1993.

Tocqueville, Alexis de. *Democracy in America*. Schocken Books, 1961.

Von Hallberg, Robert. *American Poetry and Culture, 1945–1980*. Harvard University Press, 1985.

Wallace, Ronald. *Vital Signs: Contemporary American Poetry from the University Presses*. University of Wisconsin Press, 1989.

Wright, James. "The Delicacy of Walt Whitman." In *Collected Prose.* University of Michigan Press, 1983.

———. "Poetry Must Think." In *Collected Prose.* University of Michigan Press, 1983.

Zweig, Paul. "American Poetry Restored." Review of *A Revolution in Taste. New York Times,* 17 December 1978. (Also reprinted in *On Louis Simpson,* ed. Hank Lazer. University of Michigan Press, 1988.)

———. "The New Surrealism." In *Contemporary Poetry in America,* ed. Robert Boyers. Schocken Books, 1974.

First Decade

Early Supper

Laughter of children brings
    The kitchen down with laughter.
While the old kettle sings
Laughter of children brings
To a boil all savory things.
    Higher than beam or rafter,
Laughter of children brings
    The kitchen down with laughter.

So ends an autumn day,
    Light ripples on the ceiling,
Dishes are stacked away;
So ends an autumn day,
The children jog and sway
    In comic dances wheeling.
So ends an autumn day,
    Light ripples on the ceiling.

They trail upstairs to bed,
    And night is a dark tower.
The kettle calls: instead
They trail upstairs to bed,
Leaving warmth, the coppery-red
    Mood of their carnival hour.
They trail upstairs to bed,
    And night is a dark tower.

Barbara Howes, 1959

The Blue Garden

    Blue: aconite, deadly;
Iris, a grape
Hyacinth, or tulip
    Bulb lives deep
    Down under; in March
    They drill up through that frozen

Turf.—
Blue often reverts to magenta.

Blue: larkspur
　　　　Sets its annual
Poisonous
Sights at six feet;—each
Year the
　　　　Delphinium, too,
　　　　　　Kills lice;
And both revert to magenta.

Blue: the delicate fringed
　　　　　　Gentian is a rarity
　　　　　　To be protected,
As gentian
Violet is either
　　　　　　Elegance or tincture;
Still, these too can revert to magenta.

Blue: cornflowers
　　　　　　Secure in their August
　　　　　　Field, like bachelor's
Buttons, asters—reliable
　　　　　　As wheat—return
　　　　　　For their violet season;
What tone is magenta?

It must be autumn's
　　　　Color: camouflage: white-
Tailed deer, red maples
Drying, that brown hawk diving
　　　　　　Grey as a pellet: a hodgepodge
　　　　　　Of pigment; middle-
　　　　　　Age has its own hue,
Which can easily revert to magenta.

Even so, our yarn of blood
　　　　　　Knits us together,
　　　　　　Working
Its own narrative . . .
　　　　　　This color may hold—blue

As some eyes are—and not
Revert, but keep cobalt, cobalt.

Barbara Howes, 1972

Jim Desterland

As I was fishing off Pondy Point
Between the dies, the sea so still—
Only a whisper against the boat—
No other sound but the scream of a gull,
I heard the voice you will never hear
Filling the crannies of the air.

The doors swung open, the little doors,
The door, the hatch within the brain,
And like the bellowing of ruin
The surf upon the thousand shores
Swept through me, and the thunder-noise
Of all the waves of all the seas.

The doors swung shut, the little doors,
The door, the hatch within the ear,
And I was fishing off Pondy Pier,
And all was as it was before,
With only the whisper of the swell
Against the boat, and the cry of a gull.

I draw a sight from tree to tree
Crossing this other from knoll to rock,
To mark the place. Into the sea
My line falls with an empty hook,
Yet fools the world. So day and night
I crouch upon the thwarts and wait.

There is a roaring in the skies
The great globes make, and there is the sound
Of all the atoms whirling round
That one can hear if one is wise—
Wiser than most—if one has heard
The doors, the little doors, swing wide.

Hyam Plutzik, 1959

The Premonition

Trying to imagine a poem of the future,
I saw a nameless jewel lying
Lurid on a table of black velvet.

Light winked there like eyes half-lidded,
Raying the dark with signals,
Lunar, mineral, maddening

As that white night-flower herself,
And with her delusive chastity.

Then one said: "I am the poet of the damned.
My eyes are seared with the darkness that you willed me.
This jewel is my heart, which I no longer need."

Hyam Plutzik, 1959

I Dreamed That in a City Dark as Paris

I dreamed that in a city dark as Paris
I stood alone in a deserted square.
The night was trembling with a violet
Expectancy. At the far edge it moved
And rumbled; on that flickering horizon
The guns were pumping color in the sky.

There was the Front. But I was lonely here,
Left behind, abandoned by the army.
The empty city and the empty square
Was my inhabitation, my unrest.
The helmet with its vestige of a crest,
The rifle in my hands, long out of date,
The belt I wore, the trailing overcoat
And hobnail boots, were those of a *poilu.*
I was the man, as awkward as a bear.

Over the rooftops where cathedrals loomed
In speaking majesty, two aeroplanes

Forlorn as birds, appeared. Then growing large,
The German *Taube* and the *Nieuport Scout*,
They chased each other tumbling through the sky,
Till one streamed down on fire to the earth.

These wars have been so great, they are forgotten
Like the Egyptian dynasts. My confrere
In whose thick boots I stood, were you amazed
To wander through my brain four decades later
As I have wandered in a dream through yours?

The violence of waking life disrupts
The order of our death. Strange dreams occur,
For dreams are licensed as they never were.

Louis Simpson, 1959

Landscape with Barns

The barns like scarlet lungs are breathing in
Pneumonia. The North wind smells of iron.
It's winter on the farm. The Hupmobile
That broke its back is dying at the fence.
At night in a thin house we watch TV
While moonlight falls in silence, drop by drop.

The country that Columbus thought he found
Is called America. It looks unreal,
Unreal in winter and unreal in summer.
When movies spread their giants on the air
The boys drive to the next town, drunk on nothing.
Youth has the secret. Only death looks real.

We never die. When we are old we vanish
Into the basement where we have our hobbies.
Enough, when something breaks, that widows mourn
"He would have fixed it. He knew what to do."
And life is always borrowing and lending
Like a good neighbor. How can we refuse?

Louis Simpson, 1959

Carentan O Carentan

Trees in the old days used to stand
And shape a shady lane
Where lovers wandered hand in hand
Who came from Carentan.

This was the shining green canal
Where we came two by two
Walking at combat-interval.
Such trees we never knew.

The day was early June, the ground
Was soft and bright with dew.
Far away the guns did sound,
But here the sky was blue.

The sky was blue, but there a smoke
Hung still above the sea
Where the ships together spoke
To towns we could not see.

Could you have seen us through a glass
You would have said a walk
Of farmers out to turn the grass,
Each with his own hay-fork.

The watchers in their leopard suits
Waited till it was time,
And aimed between the belt and boot
And let the barrel climb.

I must lie down at once, there is
A hammer at my knee.
And call it death or cowardice,
Don't count again on me.

Everything's alright, Mother,
Everyone gets the same
At one time or another.
It's all in the game.

I never strolled, nor ever shall,
Down such a leafy lane.
I never drank in a canal,
Nor ever shall again.

There is a whistling in the leaves
And it is not the wind,
The twigs are falling from the knives
That cut men to the ground.

Tell me, Master-Sergeant,
The way to turn and shoot.
But the Sergeant's silent
That taught me how to do it.

O Captain, show us quickly
Our place upon the map.
But the Captain's sickly
And taking a long nap.

Lieutenant, what's my duty,
My place in the platoon?
He too's a sleeping beauty,
Charmed by that strange tune.

Carentan O Carentan
Before we met with you
We never yet had lost a man
Or known what death could do.

Louis Simpson, 1959

In California

Here I am, troubling the dream coast
With my New York face,
Bearing among the realtors
And tennis-players my dark preoccupation.

There once was an epical clatter—
Voices and banjos, Tennessee, Ohio,

Rising like incense in the sight of heaven.
Today, there is an angel in the gate.

Lie back, Walt Whitman,
There on the fabulous raft with the King and the
     Duke!
For the white row of the Marina
Faces the Rock. Turn round the wagons here.

Lie back! We cannot bear
The stars any more, those infinite spaces.
Let the realtors divide the mountain,
For they have already subdivided the valley.

Rectangular city blocks astonished
Herodotus in Babylon,
Cortez in Tenochtitlan,
And here's the same old city-planner, death.

We cannot turn or stay.
For though we sleep, and let the reins fall slack,
The great cloud-wagons move
Outward still, dreaming of a Pacific.

Louis Simpson, 1963

In the Suburbs

There's no way out.
You were born to waste your life.
You were born to this middleclass life.

As others before you
Were born to walk in procession
To the temple, singing.

Louis Simpson, 1963

My Father in the Night Commanding No

My father in the night commanding No
Has work to do. Smoke issues from his lips;
    He reads in silence.
The frogs are croaking and the streetlamps glow.

And then my mother winds the gramophone;
The Bride of Lammermoor begins to shriek—
    Or reads a story
About a prince, a castle, and a dragon.

The moon is glittering above the hill.
I stand before the gateposts of the King—
    So runs the story—
Of Thule, at midnight when the mice are still.

And I have been in Thule! It has come true—
The journey and the danger of the world,
    All that there is
To bear and to enjoy, endure and do.

Landscapes, seascapes . . . where have I been led?
The names of cities—Paris, Venice, Rome—
    Held out their arms.
A feathered god, seductive, went ahead.

Here is my house. Under a red rose tree
A child is swinging; another gravely plays.
    They are not surprised
That I am here; they were expecting me.

And yet my father sits and reads in silence,
My mother sheds a tear, the moon is still,
    And the dark wind
Is murmuring that nothing ever happens.

Beyond his jurisdiction as I move
Do I not prove him wrong? And yet, it's true

They will not change
There, on the stage of terror and of love.

The actors in that playhouse always sit
In fixed positions—father, mother, child
     With painted eyes.
How sad it is to be a little puppet!

Their heads are wooden. And you once pretended
To understand them! Shake them as you will,
     They cannot speak.
Do what you will, the comedy is ended.

Father, why did you work? Why did you weep,
Mother? Was the story so important?
     "Listen!" the wind
Said to the children, and they fell asleep.

Louis Simpson, 1963

American Poetry

Whatever it is, it must have
A stomach that can digest
Rubber, coal, uranium, moons, poems.

Like the shark, it contains a shoe.
It must swim for miles through the desert
Uttering cries that are almost human.

Louis Simpson, 1963

The Troika

Troika, troika! The snow moon
whirls through the forest.

Where lamplight like a knife
gleams through a door, I see two graybeards bending.

They're playing chess, it seems. And then one rises
and stands in silence. Does he hear me passing?

Troika, troika! In the moonlight
his spirit hears my spirit passing.

I whip the horses on. The houses vanish.
The moon looks over fields
littered with debris. And there in trenches
the guardsmen stand, wind fluttering their rags.

And there were darker fields without a moon.
I walk across a field, bound on an errand.
The errand's forgotten—something depended on it.
A nightmare! I have lost my father's horses!

And then a white bird rises
and goes before me, hopping through the forest.

I held the bird—it vanished with a cry,
and on a branch a girl sat sideways, combing
her long black hair. The dew
shone on her lips; her breasts were white as roses.

Troika, troika! Three white horses,
a whip of silver, and my father's sleigh . . .

When morning breaks, the sea
gleams through the branches,
and the white bird, enchanted,
is flying through the world, across the sea.

Louis Simpson, 1963

On the Lawn at the Villa

On the lawn at the villa—
That's the way to start, eh, reader?
We know where we stand—somewhere expensive—

You and I *imperturbes*, as Walt would say,
Before the diversions of wealth, you and I *engagés*.

On the lawn at the villa
Sat a manufacturer of explosives,
His wife from Paris,
And a young man named Bruno,

And myself, being American,
Willing to talk to these malefactors,
The manufacturer of explosives, and so on,
But somehow superior. By that I mean democratic.
It's complicated, being an American,
Having the money and the bad conscience, both at
    the same time.
Perhaps, after all, this is not the right subject
    for a poem.

We were all sitting there paralyzed
In the hot Tuscan afternoon,
And the bodies of the machine-gun crew were draped
    over the balcony.
So we sat there all afternoon.

Louis Simpson, 1963

A Fit Against the Country

The stone turns over slowly,
Under the side one sees
The pale flint covered wholly
With whorls and prints of leaf.
After the moss rubs off
It gleams beneath the trees,
Till all the birds lie down.
Hand, you have held that stone.

The sparrow's throat goes hollow,
When the tense air forebodes
Rain to the sagging willow
And leaves the pasture moist.

The slow, cracked song is lost
Far up and down wet roads,
Rain drowns the sparrow's tongue.
Ear, you have heard that song.

Suddenly on the eye
Feathers of morning fall,
Tanagers float away
To sort the blackberry theft.
Though sparrows alone are left
To sound the dawn, and call
Awake the heart's gray dolor,
Eye, you have seen bright color.

Odor of fallen apple
Met you across the air,
The yellow globe lay purple
With bruises underfoot;
And, ravished out of thought,
Both of you had your share,
Sharp nose and watered mouth,
Of the dark tang of earth.

Yet, body, hold your humor
Away from the tempting tree,
The grass, the luring summer
That summon the flesh to fall.
Be glad of the green wall
You climbed across one day,
When winter stung with ice
That vacant paradise.

James Wright, 1957

At Thomas Hardy's Birthplace, 1953

1
The nurse carried him up the stair
Into his mother's sleeping room.
The beeches lashed the roof and dragged the air
      Because of storm.

Wind could have overturned the dead.
Moth and beetle and housefly crept
Under the door to find the lamp, and cowered:
    But still he slept.

The ache and sorrow of darkened earth
Left pathways soft and meadows sodden;
The small Frome overflowed the firth,
    And he lay hidden

In the arms of the tall woman gone
To soothe his mother during the dark;
Nestled against the awkward flesh and bone
    When the rain broke.

2

Last night at Stinsford where his heart
Is buried now, the rain came down.
Cold to the hidden joy, the secret hurt,
    His heart is stone.

But over the dead leaves in the wet
The mouse goes snooping, and the bird.
Something the voiceless earth does not forget
    They come to guard,

Maybe, the heart who would not tell
Whatever secret he learned from the ground,
Who turned aside and heard the human wail,
    That other sound.

More likely, though, the laboring feet
Of fieldmouse, hedgehog, moth and hawk
Seek in the storm what comfort they can get
    Under the rock

Where surely the heart will not wake again
To endure the unending beat of the air,
Having been nursed beyond the sopping rain,
    Back down the stair.

James Wright, 1959

Saint Judas

When I went out to kill myself, I caught
A pack of hoodlums beating up a man.
Running to spare his suffering, I forgot
My name, my number, how my day began,
How soldiers milled around the garden stone
And sang amusing songs; how all that day
Their javelins measured crowds; how I alone
Bargained the proper coins, and slipped away.

Banished from heaven, I found this victim beaten,
Stripped, kneed, and left to cry. Dropping my rope
Aside, I ran, ignored the uniforms:
Then I remembered bread my flesh had eaten,
The kiss that ate my flesh. Flayed without hope,
I held the man for nothing in my arms.

James Wright, 1959

Lying in a Hammock
at William Duffy's Farm
in Pine Island, Minnesota

Over my head, I see the bronze butterfly,
Asleep on the black trunk,
Blowing like a leaf in green shadow.
Down the ravine behind the empty house,
The cowbells follow one another
Into the distances of the afternoon.
To my right,
In a field of sunlight between two pines,
The droppings of last year's horses
Blaze up into golden stones.
I lean back, as the evening darkens and comes on.
A chicken hawk floats over, looking for home.
I have wasted my life.

James Wright, 1963

Autumn Begins in Martins Ferry, Ohio

In the Shreve High football stadium,
I think of Polacks nursing long beers in Tiltonsville,
And gray faces of Negroes in the blast furnace at Benwood,
And the ruptured night watchman of Wheeling Steel,
Dreaming of heroes.

All the proud fathers are ashamed to go home.
Their women cluck like starved pullets,
Dying for love.

Therefore,
Their sons grow suicidally beautiful
At the beginning of October,
And gallop terribly against each other's bodies.

James Wright, 1963

A Blessing

Just off the highway to Rochester, Minnesota,
Twilight bounds softly forth on the grass.
And the eyes of those two Indian ponies
Darken with kindness.
They have come gladly out of the willows
To welcome my friend and me.
We step over the barbed wire into the pasture
Where they have been grazing all day, alone.
They ripple tensely, they can hardly contain their happiness
That we have come.
They bow shyly as wet swans. They love each other.
There is no loneliness like theirs.
At home once more,
They begin munching the young tufts of spring in the darkness.
I would like to hold the slenderer one in my arms,
For she has walked over to me
And nuzzled my left hand.
She is black and white,
Her mane falls wild on her forehead,
And the light breeze moves me to caress her long ear

That is delicate as the skin over a girl's wrist.
Suddenly I realize
That if I stepped out of my body I would break
Into blossom.

James Wright, 1963

Two Poems about President Harding

One: His Death
In Marion, the honey locust trees are falling.
Everybody in town remembers the white hair,
The campaign of a lost summer, the front porch
Open to the public, and the vaguely stunned smile
Of a lucky man.

"Neighbor, I want to be helpful," he said once.
Later, "You think I'm honest, don't you?"
Weeping drunk.

I am drunk this evening in 1961,
In a jag for my countryman,
Who died of crab meat on the way back from Alaska.
Everyone knows that joke.

How many honey locusts have fallen,
Pitched rootlong into the open graves of strip mines,
Since the First World War ended
And Wilson the gaunt deacon jogged sullenly
Into silence?
Tonight,
The cancerous ghosts of old con men
Shed their leaves.
For a proud man,
Lost between the turnpike near Cleveland
And the chiropractors' signs looming among dead mulberry trees,
There is no place left to go
But home.

"Warren lacks mentality," one of his friends said.

Yet he was beautiful, he was the snowfall
Turned to white stallions standing still
Under dark elm trees.

He died in public. He claimed the secret right
To be ashamed.

Two: His Tomb in Ohio
". . . he died of a busted gut."—*Mencken, on Bryan*
A hundred slag piles north of us,
At the mercy of the moon and rain,
He lies in his ridiculous
Tomb, our fellow citizen.
No, I have never seen that place,
Where many shadows of faceless thieves
Chuckle and stumble and embrace
On beer cans, stogie butts, and graves.

One holiday, one rainy week
After the country fell apart,
Hoover and Coolidge came to speak
And snivel about his broken heart.
His grave, a huge absurdity,
Embarrassed cops and visitors.

Hoover and Coolidge crept away
By night, and women closed their doors.

Now junkmen call their children in
Before they catch their death of cold;
Young lovers let the moon begin
Its quick spring; and the day grows old;
The mean one-legger who rakes up leaves
Has chased the loafers out of the park;
Minnegan Leonard half-believes
In God, and the poolroom goes dark;

America goes on, goes on
Laughing, and Harding was a fool.
Even his big pretentious stone
Lays him bare to ridicule.
I know it. But don't look at me.

By God, I didn't start this mess.
Whatever moon and rain may be,
The hearts of men are merciless.

James Wright, 1963

Outside Fargo, North Dakota

Along the sprawled body of the derailed
      Great Northern freight car,
I strike a match slowly and lift it slowly.
No wind.

Beyond town, three heavy white horses
Wade all the way to their shoulders
In a silo shadow.

Suddenly the freight car lurches.
The door slams back, a man with a flashlight
Calls me good evening.
I nod as I write good evening, lonely
And sick for home.

James Wright, 1968

The Old WPA Swimming Pool
in Martins Ferry, Ohio

I am almost afraid to write down
This thing. I must have been,
Say, seven years old. That afternoon,
The families of the WPA had come out
To have a good time celebrating
A long gouge in the ground,
That the fierce husbands
Had filled with concrete.

We knew even then the Ohio
River was dying.

Most of the good men who lived along that shore
Wanted to be in love and give good love
To beautiful women, who weren't pretty,
And to small children like me who wondered,
What the hell is this?

When people don't have quite enough to eat
In August, and the river,
That is supposed to be some holiness,
Starts dying,

They swim in the earth. Uncle Sherman,
Uncle Willie, Uncle Emerson, and my father
Helped dig that hole in the ground.

I had seen by that time two or three
Holes in the ground,
And you know what they were.

But this one was not the usual, cheap
Economics, it was not the solitary
Scar on a poor man's face, that respectable
Hole in the ground you used to be able to buy
After you died for seventy-five dollars and
Your wages tached for six months by the Heslop
Brothers.

Brothers, dear God.

No, this hole was filled with water,
And suddenly I flung myself into the water.
All I had on was a jockstrap my brother stole
From a miserable football team.

Oh never mind, Jesus Christ, my father
And my uncles dug a hole in the ground,
No grave for once. It is going to be hard
For you to believe; when I rose from that water,

A little girl who belonged to somebody else,
A face thin and haunted appeared

Over my left shoulder, and whispered, Take care now,
Be patient, and live.

I have loved you all this time,
And didn't even know
I am alive.

James Wright, 1973

Redwings

It turns out
You can kill them.
It turns out
You can make the earth absolutely clean.

My nephew has given my younger brother
A scientific report while they both flew
In my older brother's small airplane
Over the Kokosing River, that looks

Secret, it looks like the open
Scar turning gray on the small
Of your spine.

Can you hear me?

It was only in the evening I saw a few redwings
Come out and dip their brilliant yellow
Bills in their scarlet shoulders.
Ohio was already going to hell.
But sometimes they would sit down on the creosote
Soaked pasture fence posts.
They used to be few, they used to be willowy and thin.

One afternoon, along the Ohio, where the sewer
Poured out, I found a nest,
The way they build their nests in the reeds,
So beautiful,
Redwings and solitaries.
The skinny girl I fell in love with down home

In late autumn married
A strip miner in late autumn.
Her five children are still alive,
Floating near the river.

Somebody is on the wing, somebody
Is wondering right at this moment
How to get rid of us, while we sleep.

Together among the dead gorges
Of highway construction, we flare
Across highways and drive
Motorists crazy, we fly
Down home to the river.

There, one summer evening, a dirty man
Gave me a nickel and a potato
And fell asleep by a fire.

James Wright, 1977

The Journey

Anghiari is medieval, a sleeve sloping down
A steep hill, suddenly sweeping out
To the edge of a cliff, and dwindling.
But far up the mountain, behind the town,
We too were swept out, out by the wind,
Alone with the Tuscan grass.

Wind had been blowing across the hills
For days, and everything now was graying gold
With dust, everything we saw, even
Some small children scampering along a road,
Twittering Italian to a small caged bird.

We sat beside them to rest in some brushwood,
And I leaned down to rinse the dust from my face.

I found the spider web there, whose hinges
Reeled heavily and crazily with the dust,

Whole mounds and cemeteries of it, sagging
And scattering shadows among shells and wings.
And then she stepped into the center of air
Slender and fastidious, the golden hair
Of daylight along her shoulders, she poised there,
While ruins crumbled on every side of her.
Free of the dust, as though a moment before
She had stepped inside the earth, to bathe herself.

I gazed, close to her, till at last she stepped
Away in her own good time.

Many men
Have searched all over Tuscany and never found
What I found there, the heart of the light
Itself shelled and leaved, balancing
On filaments themselves falling. The secret
Of this journey is to let the wind
Blow its dust all over your body,
To let it go on blowing, to step lightly, lightly
All the way through your ruins, and not to lose
Any sleep over the dead, who surely
Will bury their own, don't worry.

James Wright, 1982

My Parents En Route

Dead to the world in love my parents lie,
Snoring, and solemn as princes catafalqued,
Their dreaming toes turned upward to the sky.

Heavy with sleepy beauty, my mother walked
Last night, in her dream, in a world unknown
To me, to her, or to my father; she talked,
In that landscape, though mutely as a stone,
In colloquy with princesses of state
More marvelous than any that has been,
Waking. This of her dream I would relate.

My father, brave without fierceness, I have seen,
As after the golden tawny-yellow beast he went,

The mightiest hunter, emblazoned with exploits brave,
No fear in his look, but pity, and brave content;
My father was sent to chase that beast and have
The colloquy stately and endless argument
Of the hunt. Thus through his dream did he move.

I think, of their bedclothes' tangle and humble sleep
I make up a legend, though false as their dream
Yet true as their bodies' submissions. The steep
Sea shudders and wallows as, snoring, they steam,
Laborious ships that I love, to the deep
Tideless center and pitch of my filial dream.

David Ferry, 1960

The Soldier

Saturday afternoon. The barracks is almost empty.
The soldiers are almost all on overnight pass.
There is only me, writing this letter to you,
And one other soldier, down at the end of the room,
And a spider, that hangs by the thread of his guts,
His tenacious and delicate guts, Swift's spider,
All self-regard, or else all privacy.
The dust drifts in the sunlight around him, as currents
Lie in lazy drifting schools in the vast sea.
In his little sea the spider lowers himself
Out of his depth. He is his own diving bell,
Though he cannot see well. He observes no fish,
And sees no wonderful things. His unseeing guts
Are his only hold on the world outside himself.
I love you, and miss you, and I find you hard to imagine.
Down at the end of the room, the other soldier
Is getting ready, I guess, to go out on pass.
He is shining his boots. He sits on the edge of his bunk,
Private, submissive, and heedful of himself,
And, bending over himself, he is his own nest.
The slightest sound he makes is of his being.
He is his mother, and nest, wife, brother, and father.
His boots are bright already, yet still he rubs

And rubs till, brighter still, they are his mirror.
And in this mirror he observes, I guess,
His own submissiveness. He is far from home.

David Ferry, 1960

Three Darks Come Down Together

Three darks come down together,
Three darks close in around me:
Day dark, year dark, dark weather.

They whisper and conspire,
They search me and they sound me
Hugging my private fire.

Day done, year done, storm blowing,
Three darknesses impound me
With dark of white snow snowing.

Three darks gang up to end me,
To browbeat and dumbfound me.
Three future lights defend me.

Robert Francis, 1960

Blue Jay

So bandit-eyed, so undovelike a bird
to be my pastoral father's favorite—
skulker and blusterer
whose every arrival is a raid.

Love made the bird no gentler
nor him who loved less gentle.
Still, still the wild blue feather
brings my mild father.

Robert Francis, 1960

Dog-Day Night

Just before night darkens to total night
A child at the next farm is calling, calling,
Calling her dog. Heat and the death of wind
Bring the small wailing like a mosquito close.
Will nothing stop her? Yet my complaining adds
To my complaint. Welcome it like a bird,
A whippoorwill, I say, closing my windows
North and east. The voice evades the glass.
She will not, will not let the dog be lost.
Why don't they tell her, isn't she old enough
To hear how the whole dog-gone earth is loose
And snooping through the dark and won't come home?

Robert Francis, 1960

The Poet at Seven

And on the porch, across the upturned chair,
The boy would spread a dingy counterpane
Against the length and majesty of the rain,
And on all fours crawl in it like a bear
To lick his wounds in secret, in his lair;
And afterwards, in the windy yard again,
One hand cocked back, release his paper plane
Frail as a May fly to the faithless air.
And summer evenings he would whirl around
Faster and faster till the drunken ground
Rose up to meet him; sometimes he would squat
Among the foul weeds of the vacant lot,
Waiting for dusk and someone dear to come
And whip him down the street, but gently, home.

Donald Justice, 1960

Here in Katmandu

We have climbed the mountain.
There's nothing more to do.
It is terrible to come down
To the valley
Where, amidst many flowers,
One thinks of snow,

As, formerly, amidst snow,
Climbing the mountain,
One thought of flowers,
Tremulous, ruddy with dew,
In the valley.
One caught their scent coming down.

It is difficult to adjust, once down,
To the absence of snow.
Clear days, from the valley,
One looks up at the mountain.
What else is there to do?
Prayer wheels, flowers!

Let the flowers
Fade, the prayer wheels run down.
What have these to do
With us who have stood atop the snow
Atop the mountain,
Flags seen from the valley?

It might be possible to live in the valley,
To bury oneself among flowers,
If one could forget the mountain,
How, never once looking down,
Stiff blinded with snow,
One knew what to do.

Meanwhile it is not easy here in Katmandu,
Especially when to the valley
That wind which means snow

Elsewhere, but here means flowers,
Comes down,
As soon it must, from the mountain.

Donald Justice, 1960

On a Painting by Patient B of the Independence State Hospital for the Insane

1
These seven houses have learned to face one another,
But not at the expected angles. Those silly brown lumps,
That are probably meant for hills and not other houses,
After ages of being themselves, though naturally slow,
Are learning to be exclusive without offending.
The arches and entrances (down to the right out of sight)
Have mastered the lesson of remaining closed.
And even the skies keep a certain understandable distance,
For these are the houses of the very rich.

2
One sees their children playing with leopards, tamed
At great cost, or perhaps it is only other children,
For none of these objects is anything more than a spot,
And perhaps there are not any children but only leopards
Playing with leopards, and perhaps there are only the spots.
And the little maids that hang from the windows like tongues,
Calling the children in, admiring the leopards,
Are the dashes a child might represent motion by means of,
Or dazzlement possibly, the brilliance of solid-gold houses.

3
The clouds resemble those empty balloons in cartoons
Which approximate silence. These clouds, if clouds they are
(And not the smoke from the seven aspiring chimneys),
The more one studies them the more it appears
They too have expressions. One might almost say
They have their habits, their wrong opinions, that their

Impassivity masks an essentially lovable foolishness,
And they will be given names by those who live under them
Not public like mountains' but private like companions'.

Donald Justice, 1960

Houses

Time and the weather wear away
The houses that our fathers built.
Their ghostly furniture remains:
All the sad sofas we have stained
With tears of boredom and of guilt,

The fraying mottoes, the stopped clocks . . .
And still sometimes these tired shapes
Haunt the damp parlors of the heart.
What Sunday prisons they recall!
And what miraculous escapes!

Donald Justice, 1967

Variations for Two Pianos

For Thomas Higgins, pianist

There is no music now in all Arkansas.
Higgins is gone, taking both his pianos.

Movers dismantled the instruments, away
Sped the vans. The first detour untuned the strings.

There is no music now in all Arkansas.

Up Main Street, past the cold shopfronts of Conway,
The brash, self-important brick of the college,

Higgins is gone, taking both his pianos.

Warm evenings, the windows open, he would play
Something of Mozart's for his pupils, the birds.

There is no music now in all Arkansas.

How shall the mockingbird mend her trill, the jay
His eccentric attack, lacking a teacher?

Higgins is gone, taking both his pianos.
There is no music now in all Arkansas.

Donald Justice, 1967

Men at Forty

Men at forty
Learn to close softly
The doors to rooms they will not be
Coming back to.

At rest on a stair landing,
They feel it moving
Beneath them now like the deck of a ship,
Though the swell is gentle.

And deep in mirrors
They rediscover
The face of the boy as he practices tying
His father's tie there in secret

And the face of that father,
Still warm with the mystery of lather.
They are more fathers than sons themselves now.
Something is filling them, something

That is like the twilight sound
Of the crickets, immense,
Filling the woods at the foot of the slope
Behind their mortgaged houses.

Donald Justice, 1967

Bus Stop

Lights are burning
In quiet rooms
Where lives go on
Resembling ours.

The quiet lives
That follow us—
These lives we lead
But do not own—

Stand in the rain
So quietly
When we are gone,
So quietly . . .

And the last bus
Comes letting dark
Umbrellas out:
Black flowers, black flowers.

And lives go on.
And lives go on
Like sudden lights
At street corners

Or like the lights
In quiet rooms
Left on for hours,
Burning, burning.

Donald Justice, 1967

Adam's Footprint

Once as a child I loved to hop
On round plump bugs and make them stop
Before they crossed a certain crack.
My bantam brawn could turn them back,

My crooked step wrenched straight to kill
Live pods that then screwed tight and still.

Small sinner, stripping boughs of pears,
Shinnied past sweet and wholesome airs,
How could a tree be so unclean?
Nobody knows but Augustine.
He nuzzled pears for dam-sin's dugs—
And I scrunched roly-poly bugs.

No wolf's imprint or tiger's trace
Does Christ hunt down to catch with grace
In nets of love the devious preys
Whose feet go softly all their days:
The foot of Adam leaves the mark
Of some child scrabbling in the dark.

Vassar Miller, 1960

Aubade

I press against the emptiness
and pray the air into a shape
which dreams will not shore up.

I listen to my next-door neighbor
scuffling about like a dry leaf.
She once had a body

like mine that, rotting with its ripeness,
falls from the branch of morning to
sullen floor of sleep.

Vassar Miller, 1963

Remembering Aunt Helen

Dimly remembering how your life made
pious abstractions dance in flesh and blood
and stern negation gentle to a child—

my heart breaks into rainbows of hosannas
hovering around the memory of your head.
Remembering how somebody said, "Why, Helen
could ask me anything. I wouldn't mind."
I see that even timid hearts take courage
Under the uncondemning gaze of kindness.
Remembering how you told a little boy
who asked to buy your cat, "Honey, we don't
sell what we love," I think how most old maids'
affection for their pets is loneliness,
while yours was charity. The daily dust
your footstep stirred became a cloud of glory.
The dust I kick up irritates the nose.
What shall I do then? Shun strong drink as you did?
Read Scripture every night? Keep Sunday strictly?
Or practice with a different set of gimmicks?
Eat fish on Friday? Go to Mass each morning?
Or else fall into trances? Speak in tongues?
Remembering you, I think not. Although poets
grow beards, get drunk, and go to bed unmarried,
their imitators pull the selfsame antics
and never make it, because poems never
spring out of opium. So sanctity
changes its wardrobe at the wearer's will
not to be copied by poor little oddballs
playing their games of holy-holy-holy.
Remembering you, I weep because I find
the skirts discarded but the dancer vanished.

Vassar Miller, 1968

Ezra Pound and Robert Bridges

"We'll get 'em all back," said Robert Bridges—
Apollo, the second person singular,
Borrowed ladies, nightingales, all our outrageous
Tricks of diction, the troubadour's flair
For carefully premeditated song—
So the Laureate, marveling at Pound's courageous

Archaisms. "The world is singing on one lung.
Well away, lad, may your style be contagious."

Pound gave him the horselaugh. But Philomela,
He knew in his heart, never had it so good,
Her mother tongue ripped out, her true tralala
Decoded bluntly by the reader's blood:
Pursue the Immortal like a passing craze.
Despite slick typestrokes of your Smith-Corona
Compose in the sequence of the musical phrase.
Lo! that vacant balcony in Verona.

Robert Bagg, 1961

Death at Pocono Lake Preserve

The lifeguard's parallel simian arms
Paused by his side, then bore down on the boy's back
To teach those lungs a cadence they had known
For years.
              Sometimes his eyelash flickered just
Too delicately for us to glimpse the eye.
He loved playing on our peripheries.
The people on the lawn wept and marveled:
The slight hesitant child had boldly drowned.
He'd roamed the edge of people, animals,
And water, shedding manners like hot clothes.
One afternoon he followed me around
Spitting at my attention, then skipped and ran,
Tugging me like a fitful spaniel
Behind some old abandoned horseshoe pits,
Where a blind dying hound sat in a whir
Of insects, his yellowed tongue unfurling
Like flypaper. The child's eyewater flowed
Faster than he could see through, and I sensed
The hound, the bouncing insects and myself blurring
Into each other. We poked the animal
With sticks, and shooed the flies, but couldn't stand
To see him struggling at standing, like a foal.

With plumes of cotton out his nose, he lay,
And grew a faint grin. We expected him

To put both palms down on that slight left knee
And push himself dizzily to his feet.
We took to running hands over our legs
Watching the child lose color to the tanned sun.
From sitting so long cramped and cross-legged
My right leg fell asleep, and when I shook it
I set up maggot tingles in my nerves.
They carried him pale in a green blanket
Back to the doctor's office, by good fortune
Not fifty yards away. As it got dark
We lay on the damp grass imagining.
"I'd like to see what's going on in there,"
McCornack said. "By climbing on the skylight
Crash through and I'd land splash on his stomach,
Whoosh all the water out, rise a wet hero."

No word from inside. Night birds nudged the ground.
Occasionally a thrush would drop down hard
And stick, just like a dead ball that won't bounce.
A few at a time people left the lawn.
Stars lighting on and off, dim then brilliant
As fireflies, when my eyes moved in the pines,
Lit up his face thrilled with a mason jar
We'd filled with fireflies caught in our cupped palms.
"Look, we're outside the universe, looking
In," I told him, as those phosphorous bellies
Swelled to their nervous super novae.
I pictured his curious far-off face. Stars
Blinked in the inquisition of his eyes.

When I went to bed later on that night
I tried holding my breath, tried to imagine
Clandestine pleasures of unconsciousness
His eyes would not relinquish to my glower,
And failed. I was self-conscious of his death.
His body floated face down on my dreams.
Mosquitoes touched my arms with a soft tickle
But sucked pain suddenly. I slapped my skin
And smeared wet blood, felt the hard welts of flesh
And grew tired, happy now in heavy sweet
Safeties of sleep I felt chirring overhead.
If only I could feel how it was not

To feel, my nerve ends limp, eyes unillumined,
Nights immersing me in numb black water,
Myself forgetting myself in the blank wash,
But bitterly I warmed to wakefulness
As vague bites localized in fitful points.
I wore my discomforts thin as my skin
Envying him, in whom flies and mosquitoes
Had no interest, pallid of brow and blood,
Whose senses spilled like water off the dam,
Who left me all alone with all this life.

Dead friend, you freed the dim bad bugs of night
Convening now above my bundled head
In terrible skirls and ruined drones.
They all will spend their minutes on my skin
Except your fireflies, live and aloof as stars.

Robert Bagg, 1961

A Fit of Something Against Something

For John Ashbery

In the burgeoning age of Arnaut when for God and man to be
Shone a glory not a symptom, poetry was not austere.
Complicated laws it followed, generosity through order,
Dowered acrobats with hoops trapezing laurels undergone.
Fountainlike gyrations earned the free trouvère the name of master,
And the climax of his daring was the dazzling sestina.

When love the subject-object of Romance sestina
Left gay Provence for learned Italy to be
The guide and guard and graveyard of a supreme master,
The plaything followed, intricate turned more austere,
And doubled in and on its tracks, now woebegone
Began to learn its place and kiss the rod of order.

Petrarch and Sidney, time's woodsmen, reorder
To pastoral the still pregnant sestina
With history and logic come to be
The inspissations of its present master

Landscapes that turn upon themselves have gone
To shape a shining surface to austere.

The pious young would be austere;
They pant and puff pursuing order
(Within a shorter-breathed sestina
The fewer true). Those that have gone
The masturbatory course must be
In doubt if they or it is master.

New rebels will not master
Forms pointlessly austere.
They feel that they will be
Screwed by that alien order,
That Gestapo sestina,
Cats, it's the most ungone.

Its zing's all gone,
It's no master.
Get lost, sestina,
Go way, austere.
You'll always be
Out of order.

Sestina order,
Austere master,
BE GONE! ! !

Alan Ansen, 1961

Walt Whitman in the Civil War Hospitals

Prescient, my hands soothing
their foreheads, by my love
I earn them. In their presence
I am wretched as death. They smile
to me of love. They cheer me
and I smile. These are stones
in the catapulting world;
they fly, bury themselves in flesh,
in a wall, in earth; in midair

break against each other
and are without sound.
I sent them catapulting.
They outflew my voice
towards vacant spaces,
but I have called them farther,
to the stillness beyond,
to death which I have praised.

David Ignatow, 1961

Figures of the Human

My love, pills in her purse,
runs, now staggering, now flushed,
her speech racing near the world:
whisper talk to it, dangling,
"Let creatures ride her, soften hard bumps
for them." Who warns her from self,
racing, singing, lightfooted?
Birds, dogs, cats screech, bark, mew,
conversant with air.
                            Raise her from swooning,
the childhood spirit. Catch her
skittering, mewing with joy, barking delirium.
Then are we loved, hand drawing swiftly
figures of the human struggling awake.

David Ignatow, 1964

Rescue the Dead

Finally, to forgo love is to kiss a leaf,
is to let rain fall nakedly upon your head,
is to respect fire,
is to study man's eyes and his gestures
as he talks,
is to set bread upon the table
and a knife discreetly by,
is to pass through crowds

like a crowd of oneself.
Not to love is to live.

To love is to be led away
into a forest where the secret grave
is dug, singing, praising darkness
under the trees.

To live is to sign your name,
is to ignore the dead,
is to carry a wallet
and shake hands.

To love is to be a fish.
My boat wallows in the sea.
You who are free,
rescue the dead.

David Ignatow, 1968

The Refuse Man

I'm going to pull my stinking wagon
through the streets and countryside,
letting it smell up the highways
and its odor crawl into the one-
and two-family houses along the road
and over the corn and wheat fields
and let the cows raise their heads
from munching to bellow their anger
and the cop to draw up alongside
my wagon—I'll be pulling it
between the shafts—and let this cop,
holding his nose, come over to ask
in an awed voice what the hell
it is I'm hauling and I'll tell him,
as sweetly as I can, "A dish of rotted guts,
an empty skull, a fetid breast, a swarming
belly, a corpse, a man right out
of his mother's belly given his occupation,

and I've put myself between the shafts—
a horse will not come near this;
I had to, being a man."

David Ignatow, 1975

In the Dark

I'm seated beside my phone
waiting for a call
that will tell me everything
is settled; live as you've always
wanted to, and I keep waiting.
Only nighttime brings me
to lie down, with the phone still
beside me, waiting for it
to ring in the dark.

David Ignatow, 1978

The dog barks and is for the moment a dog heard.
The child cries and is for the moment a child heard.
Also, there is the lover swearing his oath.
Silence falls on each, and the thousands
of dogs, children and lovers pass by silently.
They could be shadows.

                    There is no turning
each to the other: "We are all lovers,
love me in return; we are all children,
love me as a child," or "We are all dogs,
let us bark together in that pleasure."
They are stilled to have found themselves
among their own kind in troops of thousands,
and when one dog barks or a lover speaks
his oath or a child cries, it is passed over
as an anomaly, a pretense
at being a dog or lover or child.

David Ignatow, 1984

White-haired, I walk in on my parents
and they, in their twenties, dark-haired
and with fresh complexions, are stunned.
I have stepped out of my crib
in the room set apart from theirs
to show myself an old man
in their youth.

I cannot spare them;
I tell them grief is pure
in what there is to know
between birth and death.

I take their hands
and lead them in a circle,
locking eyes, hands, bodies
with the past in our future.

David Ignatow, 1991

The Tennis Court Oath

What had you been thinking about
the face studiously bloodied
heaven blotted region
I go on loving you like water but
there is a terrible breath in the way all of this
You were not elected president, yet won the race
All the way through fog and drizzle
When you read it was sincere the coasts
stammered with unintentional villages the
horse strains fatigued I guess . . . the calls . . .
I worry

the water beetle head
why of course reflecting all
then you redid you were breathing
I thought going down to mail this
of the kettle you jabbered as easily in the yard
you come through but
are incomparable the lovely tent

mystery you don't want surrounded the real
you dance
in the spring there was clouds

The mulatress approached in the hall—the
lettering easily visible along the edge of the *Times*
in a moment the bell would ring but there was time
for the carnation laughed here are a couple of "other"

to one in yon house

The doctor and Philip had come over the road
Turning in toward the corner of the wall his hat on
reading it carelessly as if to tell you your fears were justified
the blood shifted you know those walls
wind off the earth had made him shrink
undeniably an oboe now the young
were there there was candy
to decide the sharp edge of the garment
like a particular cry not intervening called the dog "he's coming! he's
        coming" with an emotion felt it sink into peace

there was no turning back but the end was in sight
he chose this moment to ask her in detail about her family and the others
The person. pleaded—"have more of these
not stripes on the tunic—or the porch chairs
will teach you about men—what it means"
to be one in a million pink stripe
and now could go away the three approached the doghouse
the reef. Your daughter's
dream of my son understand prejudice
darkness in the hole
the patient finished
They could all go home now the hole was dark
lilacs blowing across his face glad he brought you.

John Ashbery, 1962

Two Sonnets

1. *Dido*
The body's products become
Fatal to it. Our spit
Would kill us, but we
Die of our heat.
Though I say the things I wish to say
They are needless, their own flame conceives it.
So I am cheated of perfection.

The iodine bottle sat in the hall
And out over the park where crawled roadsters
The apricot and purple clouds were
And our blood flowed down the grating
Of the cream-colored embassy.
Inside it they had a record of "The St. Louis Blues."

2. *The Idiot*
O how this sullen, careless world
Ignorant of me is! Those rocks, those homes
Know not the touch of my flesh, nor is there one tree
Whose shade has known me for a friend.
I've wandered the wide world over.
No man I've known, no friendly beast
Has come and put its nose into my hands.
No maid has welcomed my face with a kiss.

Yet once, as I took passage
From Gibraltar to Cape Horn
I met some friendly mariners on the boat
And as we struggle to keep the ship from sinking
The very waves seemed friendly, and the sound
The spray made as it hit the front of the boat.

John Ashbery, 1962

Our Youth

Of bricks . . . Who built it? Like some crazy balloon
When love leans on us
Its nights . . . The velvety pavement sticks to our feet.
The dead puppies turn us back on love.

Where we are. Sometimes
The brick arches led to a room like a bubble, that broke when you
    entered it
And sometimes to a fallen leaf.
We got crazy with emotion, showing how much we knew.

The Arabs took us. We knew
The dead horses. We were discovering coffee,
How it is to be drunk hot, with bare feet
In Canada. And the immortal music of Chopin

Which we had been discovering for several months
Since we were fourteen years old. And coffee grounds,
And the wonder of hands, and the wonder of the day
When the child discovers her first dead hand.

Do you know it? Hasn't she
Observed you too? Haven't you been observed to her?
My, haven't the flowers been? Is the evil
In't? What window? What did you say there?

Heh? Eh? Our youth is dead.
From the minute we discover it with eyes closed
Advancing into mountain light.
Ouch . . . You will never have that young boy,

That boy with the monocle
Could have been your father
He is passing by. No, that other one,
Upstairs. He is the one who wanted to see you.

He is dead. Green and yellow handkerchiefs cover him.
Perhaps he will never rot, I see

That my clothes are dry. I will go.
The naked girl crosses the street.

Blue hampers . . . Explosions,
Ice . . . The ridiculous
Vases of porphyry. All that our youth
Can't use, that it was created for.

It's true we have not avoided our destiny
By weeding out the old people.
Our faces have filled with smoke. We escape
Down the cloud ladder, but the problem has not been solved.

John Ashbery, 1962

The Ticket

The experience of writing you these love letters . . .
Fences not concluding, nothing, no even, water in your eye, seeming
    anything
The garden in mist, perhaps, but egocentricity makes up for that, the
    winter locusts, whitened
Her hand not leading anywhere. Her head into the yard, maples, a
    stump seen through a gauze of bottles, ruptures—
You had no permission, to carry anything out, working to carry out
    the insane orders given you to raze
The box, red, funny going underground
And, being no reason suspicious, mud of the day, the plaid—I was
    near you where you want to be
Down in the little house writing you.

Though afterwards tears seem skunks
And the difficult position we in to light the world
Of awe, mush raging, the stump again
And as always before
The scientific gaze, perfume, millions, tall laugh
That was ladder though not of uncertain, innocuous truths, the felt
    branch—

To a ditch of wine and tubs, spraying the poster with blood, telegraph,
  all the time
Automatically taking the things in, that had not been spoiled, sordid.

John Ashbery, 1962

from *The New Realism*

There was calm rapture in the way she spoke
Perhaps I would get over the way the joke
Always turned against me, in the end.
The bars had been removed from all the windows
There was something quiet in the way the light entered
Her trousseau. Wine fished out of the sea—they hadn't known
We were coming relaxed forever
We stood off the land because if you get too far
From a perfume you can squeeze the life out of it
One seal came into view and then the others
Yellow in the vast sun.
A watchdog performed and they triumphed
The day was bleak—ice had replaced air
The sigh of the children to former music
Supplanting the mutt's yelps.
This was as far as she would go—
A tavern with plants.
Dynamite out over the horizon
And a sequel, and a racket. Dolphins repelling
The sand. Squads of bulldozers
Wrecked the site, and she died laughing
Because only once does prosperity let you get away
On your doorstep she used to explain
How if the returning merchants in the morning hitched the rim of the van
In the evening one must be very quick to give them the slip.
The judge knocked. The zinnias
Had never looked better—red, yellow, and blue
They were, and the forget-me-nots and dahlias
At least sixty different varieties
As the shade went up
And the ambulance came crashing through the dust
Of the new day, the moon and the sun and the stars,

And the iceberg slowly sank
In the volcano and the sea ran far away
Yellow over the hot sand, green as the green trees.

John Ashbery, 1962

Surprised by Evening

There is unknown dust that is near us,
Waves breaking on shores just over the hill,
Trees full of birds that we have never seen,
Nets drawn down with dark fish.

The evening arrives; we look up and it is there,
It has come through the nets of the stars,
Through the tissues of the grass,
Walking quietly over the asylums of the waters.

The day shall never end, we think:
We have hair that seems born for the daylight;
But, at last, the quiet waters of the night will rise,
And our skin shall see far off, as it does under water.

Robert Bly, 1962

Sunset at a Lake

The sun is sinking. Here on the pine-haunted bank, the mosquitoes fly around drowsily, and moss stands out as if it wanted to speak. Calm falls on the lake, which now seems heavier and inhospitable. Far out, rafts of ducks drift like closed eyes, and a thin line of silver caused by something invisible slowly moves toward shore in the viscous darkness under the southern bank. Only a few birds, the troubled ones, speak to the darkening roof of earth; small weeds stand abandoned, the clay is sending her gifts back to the center of the earth.

Robert Bly, 1962

Driving Toward the Lac Qui Parle River

I

I am driving; it is dusk; Minnesota.
The stubble field catches the last growth of sun.
The soybeans are breathing on all sides.
Old men are sitting before their houses on carseats
In the small towns. I am happy,
The moon rising above the turkey sheds.

II

The small world of the car
Plunges through the deep fields of the night,
On the road from Willmar to Milan.
This solitude covered with iron
Moves through the fields of night
Penetrated by the noise of crickets.

III

Nearly to Milan, suddenly a small bridge,
And water kneeling in the moonlight.
In small towns the houses are built right on the ground;
The lamplight falls on all fours in the grass.
When I reach the river, the full moon covers it;
A few people are talking low in a boat.

Robert Bly, 1962

Remembering in Oslo the Old Picture
of the Magna Carta

The girl in a house dress, pushing open the window,
Is also the fat king sitting under the oak tree,
And the garbage men, thumping their cans, are
Crows still cawing,
And the nobles are offering the sheet to the king.
One thing is also another thing, and the doomed galleons,
Hung with trinkets, hove by the coast, and in the blossoms
Of trees are still sailing on their long voyage from Spain;

I too am still shocking grain, as I did as a boy, dog tired,
And my great-grandfather steps on his ship.

Robert Bly, 1962

Night

I
If I think of a horse wandering about sleeplessly
All night on this short grass covered with moonlight,
I feel a joy, as if I had thought
Of a pirate ship ploughing through dark flowers.

II
The box elders around us are full of joy,
Obeying what is beneath them.
The lilacs are sleeping, and the plants are sleeping,
Even the wood made into a casket is asleep.

III
The butterfly is carrying loam on his wings;
The toad is bearing tiny bits of granite in his skin;
The leaves at the crown of the tree are asleep
Like the dark bits of earth at its root.

IV
Alive, we are like a sleek black water beetle,
Skating across still water in any direction
We choose, and soon to be swallowed
Suddenly from beneath.

Robert Bly, 1962

After Drinking All Night with a Friend, We Go Out in a Boat at Dawn to See Who Can Write the Best Poem

These pines, these fall oaks, these rocks,
This water dark and touched by wind—
I am like you, you dark boat,
Drifting over water fed by cool springs.

Beneath the waters, since I was a boy,
I have dreamt of strange and dark treasures,
Not of gold, or strange stones, but the true
Gift, beneath the pale lakes of Minnesota.

This morning also, drifting in the dawn wind,
I sense my hands, and my shoes, and this ink—
Drifting, as all of this body drifts,
Above the clouds of the flesh and the stone.

A few friendships, a few dawns, a few glimpses of grass,
A few oars weathered by the snow and the heat,
So we drift toward shore, over cold waters,
No longer caring if we drift or go straight.

Robert Bly, 1962

The Performance

The last time I saw Donald Armstrong
He was staggering oddly off into the sun,
Going down, of the Philippine Islands.
I let my shovel fall, and put that hand
Above my eyes, and moved some way to one side
That his body might pass through the sun,

And I saw how well he was not
Standing there on his hands,
On his spindle-shanked forearms balanced,

Unbalanced, with his big feet looming and waving
In the great, untrustworthy air
He flew in each night, when it darkened.

Dust fanned in scraped puffs from the earth
Between his arms, and blood turned his face inside out,
To demonstrate its suppleness
Of veins, as he perfected his role.
Next day, he toppled his head off
On an island beach to the south,

And the enemy's two-handed sword
Did not fall from anyone's hands
At that miraculous sight,
As the head rolled over upon
Its wide-eyed face, and fell
Into the inadequate grave

He had dug for himself, under pressure.
Yet I put my flat hand to my eyebrows
Months later, to see him again
In the sun, when I learned how he died,
And imagined him, there,
Come, judged, before his small captors,

Doing all his lean tricks to amaze them—
The back somersault, the kip-up—
And at last, the stand on his hands,
Perfect, with his feet together,
His head down, evenly breathing,
As the sun poured up from the sea

And the headsman broke down
In a blaze of tears, in that light
Of the thin, long human frame
Upside down in its own strange joy,
And, if some other one had not told him,
Would have cut off the feet

Instead of the head,
And if Armstrong had not presently risen

In kingly, round-shouldered attendance,
And then knelt down in himself
Beside his hacked, glittering grave, having done
All things in this life that he could.

James Dickey, 1957

A Screened Porch in the Country

All of them are sitting
Inside a lamp of coarse wire
And being in all directions
Shed upon darkness,
Their bodies softening to shadow, until
They come to rest out in the yard
In a kind of blurred golden country
In which they more deeply lie
Than if they were being created
Of Heavenly light.

Where they are floating beyond
Themselves, in peace,
Where they have laid down
Their souls and not known it,
The smallest creatures,
As every night they do,
Come to the edge of them
And sing, if they can,
Or, if they can't, simply shine
Their eyes back, sitting on haunches,

Pulsating and thinking of music.
Occasionally, something weightless
Touches the screen
With its body, dies,
Or is unmurmuringly hurt,
But mainly nothing happens
Except that a family continues
To be laid down

In the midst of its nightly creatures,
Not one of which openly comes

Into the golden shadow
Where the people are lying,
Emitted by their own house
So humanly that they become
More than human, and enter the place
Of small, blindly singing things,
Seeming to rejoice
Perpetually, without effort,
Without knowing why
Or how they do it.

James Dickey, 1962

Hunting Civil War Relics at Nimblewill Creek

As he moves the mine detector
A few inches over the ground,
Making it vitally float
Among the ferns and weeds,
I come into this war
Slowly, with my one brother,
Watching his face grow deep
Between the earphones,
For I can tell
If we enter the buried battle
Of Nimblewill
Only by his expression.

Softly he wanders, parting
The grass with a dreaming hand.
No dead cry yet takes root
In his clapped ears
Or can be seen in his smile.
But underfoot I feel
The dead regroup,

The burst metals all in place,
The battle lines be drawn
Anew to include us
In Nimblewill,
And I carry the shovel and pick

More as if they were
Bright weapons that I bore.
A bird's cry breaks
In two, and into three parts.
We cross the creek; the cry
Shifts into another,
Nearer, bird, and is
Like the shout of a shadow—
Lived-with, appallingly close—
Or the soul, pronouncing
"Nimblewill":
Three tones; your being changes.

We climb the bank;
A faint light glows
On my brother's mouth.
I listen, as two birds fight
For a single voice, but he
Must be hearing the grave,
In pieces, all singing
To his clamped head,
For he smiles as if
He rose from the dead within
Green Nimblewill
And stood in his grandson's shape.

No shot from the buried war
Shall kill me now,
For the dead have waited here
A hundred years to create
Only the look on the face
Of my one brother,
Who stands among them, offering
A metal dish
Afloat in the trembling weeds,

With a long-buried light on his lips
At Nimblewill
And the dead outsinging two birds.

I choke the handle
Of the pick, and fall to my knees
To dig wherever he points,
To bring up mess tin or bullet,
To go underground
Still singing, myself,
Without a sound,
Like a man who renounces war,
Or one who shall lift up the past,
Not breathing "Father,"
At Nimblewill,
But saying, "Fathers! Fathers!"

James Dickey, 1962

In the Mountain Tent

I am hearing the shape of the rain
Take the shape of the tent and believe it,
Laying down all around where I lie
A profound, unspeakable law.
I obey, and am free-falling slowly

Through the thought-out leaves of the wood
Into the minds of animals.
I am there in the shining of water
Like dark, like light, out of Heaven.

I am there like the dead, or the beast
Itself, which thinks of a poem—
Green, plausible, living, and holy—
And cannot speak, but hears,
Called forth from the waiting of things,

A vast, proper, reinforced crying
With the sifted, harmonious pause,

The sustained intake of all breath
Before the first word of the Bible.

At midnight water dawns
Upon the held skulls of the foxes
And weasels and tousled hares
On the eastern side of the mountain.
Their light is the image I make

As I wait as if recently killed,
Receptive, fragile, half-smiling,
My brow watermarked with the mark
On the wing of a moth

And the tent taking shape on my body
Like ill-fitting, Heavenly clothes.
From holes in the ground comes my voice
In the God-silenced tongue of the beasts.
"I shall rise from the dead," I am saying.

James Dickey, 1962

The Dusk of Horses

Right under their noses, the green
Of the field is paling away
Because of something fallen from the sky.

They see this, and put down
Their long heads deeper in grass
That only just escapes reflecting them

As the dream of a millpond would.
The color green flees over the grass
Like an insect, following the red sun over

The next hill. The grass is white.
There is no cloud so dark and white at once;
There is no pool at dawn that deepens

Their faces and thirsts as this does.
Now they are feeding on solid
Cloud, and, one by one,

With nails as silent as stars among the wood
Hewed down years ago and now rotten,
The stalls are put up around them.

Now if they lean, they come
On wood on any side. Not touching it, they sleep.
No beast ever lived who understood

What happened among the sun's fields,
Or cared why the color of grass
Fled over the hill while he stumbled,

Led by the halter to sleep
On his four taxed, worthy legs.
Each thinks he awakens where

The sun is black on the rooftop,
That the green is dancing in the next pasture,
And that the way to sleep

In a cloud, or in a risen lake,
Is to walk as though he were still
In the drained field standing, head down,

To pretend to sleep when led,
And thus to go under the ancient white
Of the meadow, as green goes

And whiteness comes up through his face
Holding stars and rotten rafters,
Quiet, fragrant, and relieved.

James Dickey, 1964

Buckdancer's Choice

So I would hear out those lungs,
The air split into nine levels,
Some gift of tongues of the whistler

In the invalid's bed: my mother,
Warbling all day to herself
The thousand variations of one song;

It is called Buckdancer's Choice.
For years, they have all been dying
Out, the classic buck-and-wing men

Of traveling minstrel shows;
With them also an old woman
Was dying of breathless angina,

Yet still found breath enough
To whistle up in my head
A sight like a one-man band,

Freed black, with cymbals at heel,
An ex-slave who thrivingly danced
To the ring of his own clashing light

Through the thousand variations of one song
All day to my mother's prone music,
The invalid's warbler's note,

While I crept close to the wall
Sock-footed, to hear the sounds alter,
Her tongue like a mockingbird's break

Through stratum after stratum of a tone
Proclaiming what choices there are
For the last dancers of their kind,

For ill women and for all slaves
Of death, and children enchanted at walls
With a brass-beating glow underfoot,

Not dancing but nearly risen
Through barnlike, theatrelike houses
On the wings of the buck and wing.

James Dickey, 1965

The Leap

The only thing I have of Jane MacNaughton
Is one instant of a dancing-class dance.
She was the fastest runner in the seventh grade,
My scrapbook says, even when boys were beginning
To be as big as the girls,
But I do not have her running in my mind,
Though Frances Lane is there, Agnes Fraser,
Fat Betty Lou Black in the boys-against-girls
Relays we ran at recess: she must have run

Like the other girls, with her skirts tucked up
So they would be like bloomers,
But I cannot tell; that part of her is gone.
What I do have is when she came,
With the hem of her skirt where it should be
For a young lady, into the annual dance
Of the dancing class we all hated, and with a light
Grave leap, jumped up and touched the end
Of one of the paper-ring decorations

To see if she could reach it. She could,
And reached me now as well, hanging in my mind
From a brown chain of brittle paper, thin
And muscular, wide-mouthed, eager to prove
Whatever it proves when you leap
In a new dress, a new womanhood, among the boys
Whom you easily left in the dust
Of the passionless playground. If I said I saw
In the paper where Jane MacNaughton Hill,

Mother of four, leapt to her death from a window
Of a downtown hotel, and that her body crushed-in
The top of a parked taxi, and that I held

Without trembling a picture of her lying cradled
In that papery steel as though lying in the grass,
One shoe idly off, arms folded across her breast,
I would not believe myself. I would say
The convenient thing, that it was a bad dream
Of maturity, to see that eternal process

Most obsessively wrong with the world
Come out of her light, earth-spurning feet
Grown heavy: would say that in the dusty heels
Of the playground some boy who did not depend
On speed of foot, caught and betrayed her.
Jane, stay where you are in my first mind:
It was odd in that school, at that dance.
I and the other slow-footed yokels sat in corners
Cutting rings out of drawing paper

Before you leapt in your new dress
And touched the end of something I began,
Above the couples struggling on the floor,
New men and women clutching at each other
And prancing foolishly as bears: hold on
To that ring I made for you, Jane—
My feet are nailed to the ground
By dust I swallowed thirty years ago—
While I examine my hands.

James Dickey, 1967

Coming Back to America

We descended the first night from Europe   riding the ship's sling
Into the basement.   Forty floors of home weighed on us.   We broke through
To a room, and fell to drinking madly with all those boozing, reading
The Gideon Bible in a dazzle of homecoming scripture   Assyrian armies
The scythes of chariots blazing like the windows of the city   all cast
Into our eyes in all-night squinting barbaric rays of violent unavoidable glory.
There were a "million dollars in ice cubes" outside our metal door;
The dead water clattered down hour after hour as we fought with salesmen
For the little blocks that would make whole our long savage drinks.
I took a swaying shower, and we packed the whole bathroom of towels into

Our dusty luggage, battling paid-for opulence with whatever weapon
Came to hand.   We slept; I woke up early, knowing that I was suffering
But not why. My breath would not stir, nor the room's.   I sweated
Ice in the closeness   my head hurt with the Sleep of a Thousand Lights
That the green baize drapes could not darken.   I got up, bearing
Everything   found my sharp Roman shoes   went out   following signs
That said SWIMMING POOL.   Flashing bulbs on a red-eyed panel, I passed
Through ceiling after ceiling of sleeping salesmen and whores, and came out
On the roof.   The pool water trembled with the few in their rooms
Still making love.   This was air.   A skinny girl lifeguard worked
At her nails; the dawn shone on her right leg in a healthy, twisted flame.
It made me squint   slick and lacquered with scars   with the wild smoky city
Around it   the great breath to be drawn above sleepers   the hazy
Morning towers.   We sat and talked   she said a five-car wreck
Of taxis in Bensonhurst had knocked her out and taken her kneecap
But nothing else.   I pondered this   the sun shook off a last heavy
Hotel   and she leapt and was in the fragile green pool as though
I were still sleeping it off eleven floors under her: she turned in a water
Ballet by herself—graceful   unredeemable   her tough face exactly
As beautiful and integral as the sun come out of the city.   Vulnerable,
Hurt in my country's murderous speed, she moved   and I would have taken
Her in my arms in water throbbing with the passion of travelling men,
Unkillable, both of us, at forty stories in the morning   and could have
Flown with her   our weightlessness preserved by the magic pool drawn from
Under the streets   out of that pond   passing over the meaningless
Guardrail   feeling the whole air pulse like water sleepless with desperate
Love-making   lifting us out of sleep into the city summer dawn
Of hundreds of feet of gray space spinning with pigeons now under
Us   among new panels of sun in the buildings blasting light silently
Back and forth across streets between them: could have moved with her
In all this   over the floods of glare raised up in sheets   the gauze
Distances where warehouses strove to become   over the ship I had ridden
Home in   riding gently   whitely   beneath.   Ah, lift us, green
City water, as we turn the harbor around with our legs   lazily changing
The plan of the city with motions like thistles   like the majestic swirl
Of soot   the winged seed of pigeons   and so would have held her
As I held my head   a-stammer with light   defending it against the terrible
Morning sun of drinkers   in that pain, exhalting in the blind notion
Of cradling her somewhere above ships and buses   in the air like a water
Ballet   dancing deep among the dawn buildings in a purely private
Embrace of impossibility   a love that could not have been guessed:
Woman   being   idea   temple dancer   tough girl from Bensonhurst

With a knee rebuilt out of sunlight   returned-to amazement   O claspable
Symbol   the unforeseen on home ground   The thing that sustains us forever
In other places!

James Dickey, 1967

Night Bird

Some beating in there

That has bunched, and backed
Up in it out of moonlight, and now
Is somewhere around. You are sure that like a curving grave

It must be able to fall
                            and rise
                                        and fall and that's
Right, and rise
                    on your left hand
                                        or other

Or behind your back on one hand

You don't have and suddenly there is no limit

To what a man can get out of
His failure to see:
                        this gleam

Of air down the nape of the neck, and in it everything
There is of flight
                        and nothing else,
                                        and it is

All right and all over you
From around
                    as you are carried

In yourself and there is no way
To nothing-but-walk—

No way and a bidden flurry
And a half-you of air.

James Dickey, 1990

Agreement with Sir Charles Sedley

Accommodating love with "something still
    Of the sea," he only meant
    To decorate a failure spent
Upon Corinna's bed, from which he went
Away too suddenly to serve it well.

Yet with her for an hour the Cavalier
    Discovered comfort from the cold,
    And found it politic to hold
A warming world against him, though he told
Corinna's maid to call him well before

The King would ride, and time itself return.
    The lovers closeted apace
    And fell together—an embrace
That gathered each unbidden sense to grace,
Though not the kind Corinna's fan could learn.

Thereat the summons of a little bell
    Inconsiderately spread
    Silver tumult overhead.
Corinna laughed, and tidied up her bed;
The laureate subsided with the swell.

In truth love had a semblance of the sea,
    Showing less among the fair
    Ripples of Corinna's hair
Than sharing in the ignorant and bare
Condition of its wreck: a breaking free.

Corinna stirred. She was alone, so closed
    Her cabinet. Perhaps she thought
    How Venus' beauty had been wrought
To birth upon the ocean, later caught

With Mars in Vulcan's net. Corinna dozed.

That night, at Margate, the low water ran
    White on every knocking stone,
    Embittered almost, as if one
God more were gone. It was the very tone
And timbre—somewhat louder—of a man.

Richard Howard, 1962

Seeing Cousin Phyllis Off

The SS France, *Second Class, Cabin U–20*

        Few sights were lovelier
    Than my watch laved in the *brut* champagne
    Exploding from a jiggled magnum.
Your foreign cabin-mates' *schadenfreude*
        Helped them help each other
    To more caviar, and your handsome
    Husband brushed me off, as handsome does;
Wizened by a decade of adultery,
        You whispered some final
    Instructions under the din, patted
    Your graying bun: for a dozen years
The sacred fount had been flowing in his
        Favor, and you knew it.
    In Paris, a daughter was pregnant,
    Unmarried, impatient for your next
Round of meddling to begin. The cycle
        Of all our messy lives
    Alters so little from war to war
    I wonder how any of us
Dares to hope for a private happiness.
        Wilde said what we want is
    Pleasure, not happiness—it has more
    Tragic possibilities. Your caviar
Must be second-class too: I miss the old
        Normandie, Narrenschiff
    Of our fashionable thirties. Now
    The diesels suddenly start to throb

In a sickening vibrato that drives
            The implacable screw
        Up through even the *pont supérieur.*
        My stomach turns, but all the champagne
Is gone, except for the foam in my watch,
            I nod at the nightmare
        Of a class that we both belong to:
        Repetition, and hurry away
To give your worried lover messages.
            My poor mad Cousin Phyl,
        No use trying to drown time on these
        Harridan voyages of ours—once
They called them maiden—not by wet watches
            Or even dry champagne.

Richard Howard, 1967

Ballad of Dead Yankees

Where's Babe Ruth, the King of Swat,
Who rocked the heavens with his blows?
Grabowski, Pennock, and Malone—
Mother of mercy, where are those?

Where's Tony (Poosh 'em up) Lazzeri,
The quickest man that ever played?
Where's the gang that raised the roof
In the house that Colonel Ruppert made?

Where's Lou Gehrig, strong and shy,
Who never missed a single game?
Where's Tiny Bonham, where's Jake Powell
And many another peerless name?

Where's Steve Sundra, good but late,
Who for a season had his fling?
Where are the traded, faded ones?
Lord, can they tell us anything?

Where's the withered nameless dwarf
Who sold us pencils at the gate?

Hurled past the clamor of our cheers?
Gone to rest with the good and great?

Where's the swagger, where's the strut,
Where's the style that made the hitter?
Where's the pitcher's swanlike motion?
What in God's name turned life bitter?

For strong-armed Steve, who lost control
And weighed no more than eighty pounds,
No sooner benched than in his grave,
Where's the cleverness that confounds?

For Lou the man, erect and clean,
Wracked with a cruel paralysis,
Gone in his thirty-seventh year,
Where's the virtue that was his?

For nimble Tony, cramped in death,
God knows why and God knows how,
Shut in a dark and silent house,
Where's the squirrel quickness now?

For big brash Babe in an outsize suit,
Himself grown thin and hoarse with cancer,
Still autographing balls for boys,
Mother of mercy, what's the answer?

Is there a heaven with rainbow flags,
Silver trophies hung on walls?
A horseshoe grandstand, mobs of fans,
Webbed gloves and official balls?

Is there a power in judgment there
To stand behind the body's laws,
A stern-faced czar whose slightest word
Is righteous as Judge Kenesaw's?

And if there be no turnstile gate
At that green park, can we get in?

Is the game suspended or postponed?
And do the players play to win?

Mother of mercy, if you're there,
Pray to the high celestial czar
For all of these, the early dead,
Who've gone where no ovations are.

Donald Petersen, 1964

Lovers in Summer

Near the frayed edges of towns,
      the places where roads tire
      of their coats of tar
      and shed them to run bare
      in the dust; there, paired
      lovers roll in the grass
      wrapped in halos of insects,
      wreathed by summers of loneliness.

Out in the country others pretend
      to romp in haylofts,
      mimicking the motions
      of animals, making
      themselves seem robust
      though their bones
      bear the long-planted
      seeds of rickets. Their limbs
      are bowed and thin,
      full of future fractures
      and undiscovered limps.

Elsewhere initials are carved
      in the soft bark
      of sentiment and eternal
      pledges are made.
      Nights are ripe
      with affirmations

heard through echo chambers.
And young men scratch
their knees on the pebbles
of their proposals.

Muted, perspiring, the long
        nights of adolescence
        continue in obscure
        parking places where
        engagements have been
        sealed and bruises found
        among cool leatherette.
        The marathons of their lives
        have come to this:
        they hear the parched
        runners of their blood
        approaching to light
        victory fires
        in their groins.

And everywhere in rooms
        the lamps go down,
        the record players play
        and parents strain
        near sleep to hear
        the sounds of zippers,
        the tentative noises
        of bedrooms, the voices
        of couch springs
        that accompany
        each sugary moan.

Vern Rutsala, 1964

Late at Night

Not willing to exert the mind enough even to sense the quality of the
lives of those nearest us, we will, however, late at night, create from
scratch around a few random sounds in the cellar—pipes knocking, the

furnace working—a whole human being, the prowler come to punish us
for lack of love.

Vern Rutsala, 1978

Bodies

Given their natural inclinations toward betrayal, they cannot be
trusted. They introduce foreign elements into our lives; they encourage
appetites we exhaust ourselves resisting or satisfying; or they develop
their own vices of the cells which we call disease. And since we have only
their little hands to work with, we are helpless against them.

Vern Rutsala, 1978

Night Wind in Fall

Air heaves at matter:
The wind makes all the wind noises.
Twig-strain, leaf-scatter,
Tapping of tips on rebuffing windows,
Nut-fall, little shatter
Of rotted small limbs on blunting ground.
Neither metronomic nor constant,
But recurring as metres recur.

I remember "Words alone
Are certain good." I don't hear,
Either in twig-tap, blown-
Leaf sigh, or hissing or whistle
Or scrape, the singular tone
Of a word. Inarticulate wind.
Yet a rising and falling persists.
Words are a rising and falling.

Someone less drowsy
Than I am, might understand,
Might catch, from mousy

Sounds and silences, birdlike
Alternations, from ghostly
Stutters, a viable pattern of words.
Unclogged senses might do it.
There must be senses unclogged

Somewhere. Maybe, I think,
They can decode such words
As bless, from brink to brink,
The whole reach that listens under the wind.
I hope each chink, each link
That forms this house is blessed. And all
Houses. All of the running grass.
Every lake in Canada under the stars.

W. R. Moses, 1965

Dark and Dark

Slowly now, and softly now, and sweetly
The earth in its spin carries us into communion
With the big darkness set with its dancing stars.
The small lights of the small, nearby darkness
Come on, house lamps and street lamps. But trees and hedges
Block and confuse them. My yard, like the rolling sky,
Has just enough light to declare darkness' identity.

I think of the nested thrasher out in the fence,
Closely enfolding her eggs in the grassy structure
Established between wire mesh and the thrusting limbs
Of the old wild grape that scrambles and sprawls so broadly
That it takes from the fence its nature of thin uprightness,
And makes it suggest, in the dark, some primitive longhouse,
Or perhaps an extended burial mound. I wonder

Whether the darkness enfolding the bird's awareness
Is the big darkness that dwarfs the innumerable stars,
Or only the little darkness of the fussy crust
Of earth, that is always fretting to increase the number
Of its little lights, as though it could thus deny

What lies all around it. I think that a being of the wild
Must retain the wild in its heart, however surrounded

By all the pretensions of tameness. It feels the big dark.
Grape leaves are broad; the beams of the small lights strike them
Like weak, stray arrows that glance from impervious shields.
The trunk of a hackberry rises as broad as a hill
To shelter a bird from everything lying beyond it.
The dark that contains the stars, and renders them tiny,
Contains too the bird, softly and sweetly enfolds her.

W. R. Moses, 1976

Junker-Lied

Schleswig-Holstein

More than myself (estate, degree),
I discipline my world to me,

For whom the viewpoint fills the view;
For whom all things become these few:

Four pinnacles and four clear ponds,
A quartered sky that corresponds;

The charted cattle, maps of peace,
And white ellipses which are geese.

If, in the dream's contempt of truth,
A goosegirl first is swan, then youth . . .

Awakened, would he see in mine
Seducer's eyes and base design,

Or only see what he may know,
That evil's grace is not to show.

Could he distinguish, did he try,
Which is the eyeglass, which the eye.

Turner Cassity, 1966

Epigoni Go French Line

Egalitarian and full of plastics,
S.S. France, efficient, safe, and banal.
Mirrors double in the English Channel.
One reflection has her own statistics;
One has patently an extra funnel.

She, that other, follows where the real
Distorts her; just below the water, just,
But only just, describable—her past
Already idiom, her loss detail.
Imperfectly, the structured meaning lost

And connotation gone, hers, nonetheless,
Prevail. Time is the steward of décor.
In auctioned fittings that no longer are,
Persists the image that forever is:
Ease, class on class, and in the distance, war.

Meanwhile, if enamel, glazes, metal
Bear the mark of Cain, here, being human,
It lends them what the *France* can never summon.
Simply, well aware it may be fatal,
Luxury is drive toward the uncommon.

It is for those crystal decks their caption,
Seal, or birthmark; it is where in sudden,
Brief incests of conspicuous consumption,
Action mannequins, or Wallis Simpson,
Meet fortune hunters in the Winter Garden.

It is the stainless steel piano, closed.*
Its motive of the jagged chromium,
The frozen lightning flash, forever posed
Above what portal, brands on whom they used
The shaping will and realized extreme.

And though internment, auction, fire, and scrap
May wait it, they are such *frisson*, such fear
As give it edge. To grace it with death pure,

To spare it, thus, graffiti of the troop-
ship, "Kilroy took his social vengeance here,"

Elective fire seems less than ever Hell.
The Channel clouds; the ships merge utterly;
Our faith now is in the *France,* for good or ill.
But when the bored forsake the guarding rail,
The life preserver, spotlit, still reads *Normandie.*

*The stainless steel piano was actually aluminum, and was on the *Hindenburg,* not the *Normandie.* This is known as poetic license.

Turner Cassity, 1966

The Field of the Caribou

Moving in a restless exhaustion,
humps of earth that rise
covered with dead hair.

There is no sound from the wind
blowing the tattered velvet
of their antlers.

The grey shepherds of the tundra
pass like islands of smoke,
and I hear only a heavy thumping
as though far in the west
some tired bodies
were falling from a cliff.

John Haines, 1966

The House of the Injured

I found a house in the forest,
small, windowless, and dark.

From the doorway came the close,
suffocating odor of blood
and fur mixed with dung.

I looked inside and saw an injured
bird that filled the room,
fluttering against the walls.

With a stifled croaking
it lunged toward the door
as if held back
by an invisible chain:

the beak was half eaten away,
and its heart beat wildly
under the rumpled feathers.

I sank to my knees—
a man shown the face of God.

John Haines, 1966

Dürer's Vision

The country is not named,
but it looks like home.

A scarred pasture,
thick columns of rain,
or smoke . . .

A dark, inverted mushroom
growing from the sky
into the earth.

John Haines, 1971

Choosing a Stone

It grows cold in the forest
of rubble.

There the old hunters survive
and patch their tents with tar.

They light fires in the night
of obsidian—
instead of trees they burn
old bottles and windowpanes.

Instead of axe blows and leaves
falling,
there is always the sound
of moonlight breaking,
of brittle stars ground together.

The talk there is of deadfalls
and pits armed
with splinters of glass,

and of how one chooses a stone.

John Haines, 1971

There Are No Such Trees in Alpine, California

I wanted a house
on the shore of Summer Lake,
where the cottonwoods burn
in a stillness beyond October,
their fires warming the Oregon farms.

There John Fremont and his men
rested when they came down late
from the winter plateau,
and mended in the waning sunlight.

Sprawled among frayed tents
and balky campfires, they told
of their fellowship in fever,
stories torn from buffalo tongues,
words of wind in a marrowbone;
how the scorched flower of the prairie
came to ash on a shore of salt.

Then silent and half asleep,
they gazed through green smoke

at the cottonwoods, spent leaves
caught fire and falling,
gathering more light and warmth
from the hearth of the sun,
climbing and burning again.

And there I too wanted to stay . . .
speak quietly to the trees,
tell in a notebook sewn from
their leaves my brief of passage:
long life without answering speech,
grief enforced in that absence;
much joy in the weather,
spilled blood on the snow.

With a few split boards,
a handful of straightened nails,
a rake and a broom;
my chair by the handmade window,
the stilled heart come home
through smoke and falling leaves.

John Haines, 1977

Sleep

Whether we fall asleep under the moon
like gypsies, with silver coins
in our pockets, or crawl deep
into a cave through which the warm,
furry bats go grinning and flying,
or put on a great black coat
and simply ride away into the darkness,

we become at last like trees
who stand within themselves, thinking.

And when we awake—if we do—
we come back bringing the images
of a lonely childhood: the hands

we held, the threads we unwound
from the shadows beneath us;
and sounds as of voices in another room
where some part of our life
was being prepared—near which we lay,
waiting for our life to begin.

John Haines, 1982

Mothball Fleet: Benicia, California

These massed grey shadows
of a distant war,
anchored among burnt hills.

The chained pitch and sweep of them
streaked with rust,
swinging in the sunlit silence,
hinges of a terrible labor.

Years before the last war
my father and I floated past them
on the Chesapeake:
our oarlocks and quiet voices
sounded in the hollow hulls.

And once again these shadows
crossed between me and the sunlight,
formations under flags of smoke.
They carried men, torpedoes,
sealed orders in weighted sacks,
to join tomorrow
some bleak engagement
I will not see.

They are the moving, the stationary
walls of my time.
They hold within them cries,
cold, echoing spaces.

John Haines, 1982

National Cold Storage Company

The National Cold Storage Company contains
More things than you can dream of.
Hard by the Brooklyn Bridge it stands
In a litter of freight cars,
Tugs to one side; the other, the traffic
Of the Long Island Expressway.
I myself have dropped into it in seven years
Midnight tossings, plans for escape, the shakes.
Add this to the national total—
Grant's tomb, the Civil War, Arlington,
The young President dead.
Above the warehouse and beneath the stars
The poets creep on the harp of the Bridge.
But see,
They fall into the National Cold Storage Company
One by one. The wind off the river is too cold,
Or the times too rough, or the Bridge
Is not a harp at all. Or maybe
A monstrous birth inside the warehouse
Must be fed by everything—ships, poems,
Stars, all the years of our lives.

Harvey Shapiro, 1966

For W C W

Now they are trying to make you
The genital thug, leader
Of the new black shirts—
Masculinity over all!
I remember you after the stroke
(Which stroke? I don't remember which stroke.)
Afraid to be left by Flossie
In a hotel lobby, crying out
To her not to leave you
For a minute. Cracked open
And nothing but womanish milk
In the hole. Only a year

Before that we were banging
On the door for a girl to open,
To both of us. Cracked,
Broken. Fear
Slaughtering the brightness
Of your face, stroke and
Counterstroke, repeated and
Repeated, for anyone to see.
And now, grandmotherly,
You stare from the cover
Of your selected poems—
The only face you could compose
In the end. As if having
Written of love better than any poet
Of our time, you stepped over
To that side for peace.
What valleys, William, to retrace
In memory, after the masculine mountains,
What long and splendid valleys.

Harvey Shapiro, 1971

Hello There!

For Robert Bly

The poets of the midwest
Are in their towns,
Looking out across wheat, corn,
Great acres of silos.
Neruda waves to them
From the other side of the field.
They are all so happy
They make images.

Harvey Shapiro, 1971

After the Love-making

After the love-making
in which we tasted each other
so that the colors spread and mixed
we got up quietly to prepare dinner.

The sadness of the year ending.
The dead outside my window,
that increasing company of relatives and friends.
So we are not to be herded into freight cars.
Each will have his chance at happiness.

To be able to help each other.
Is that possible?
At the end of the play
you say to me that the life we saw
has reverberations, has history.
I agree and want to say
that even our drama
is not merely personal,
though we see only the edge of the personal.
I am with you
in saying it is not enough.

Harvey Shapiro, 1984

When Sanders brings feed to his chickens, some sparrows
    Sitting and rocking in the peach tree at the fence corner
    By the chicken house, fly up
    And shoot off to another tree farther away,
    An acacia. The whole air
    Is shaken by their mass motion.

    But then one leaf of the empty peach tree stirs
    And I see in it one sparrow sitting still.
    Is he a guard? absent-minded? averse
    To mass motion? Rather, he may enjoy
    The comings and goings
    Of Sanders to the chickens.

Josephine Miles, 1967

When I was eight, I put in the left-hand drawer
    Of my new bureau a prune pit.
    My plan was that darkness and silence
    Would grow it into a young tree full of blossoms.

    Quietly and unexpectedly I opened the drawer a crack
    And looked for the sprouts; always the pit
    Anticipated my glance, and withheld
    The signs I looked for.

    After a long time, a week, I felt sorry
    For the lone pit, self-withheld,
    So saved more, and lined them up like an orchard.
    A small potential orchard of free flowers.

    Here memory and storage lingered
    Under my fingerprints past retrieval,
    Musty and impatient as a prairie
    Without its bee.

    Some friends think of this recollection
    As autobiography. Others think it
    A plausible parable of computer analysis.
    O small and flowering orchard of free friends!

Josephine Miles, 1967

Events by Moonlight

Some intense event dictated a poem;
Poem and event had come closer together than ever before.
It was as if, in passing,
The event had pressed its own image against the page.
And its very shape had left a mark

The hand lay useless on top of the desk. It smoked.

The pencil fell under the desk unsharpened and broken
And the moon rising over the very intimate room

Pressed itself very hard against the window where the groups of
   lovers had recently been assembled.

A whole landscape of future events was illuminated out there
      in the room
But none could be without the moon's being:
The dust of events was never shed on the paper except under
      the moonlight

Michael Benedikt, 1968

Dossier of the Torturer

In with the big stack of advertisements for Pain, Mole finds two inter-
esting books of differing sizes. They are useful books, too. One is a cat-
alogue of the ways people have of making each other miserable. It is
entitled *Dossier of the Torturer*. It is so full of "human" needs and re-
quirements, so full of "demands" made of others—not to mention the
techniques of extraction and pressure—so big and thick, that Mole finds
it useful as a floorboard for one whole room in the Mole-hole. The other
volume is also a catalogue, this one describing the ways people have of
bringing joy to others or to themselves. The cover identifies it as a "sex-
ual manual." Examining this book, Mole notes that in contrast to the
primitive simplicity of the most effective methods of torture, most of the
methods of pleasure are so complicated and sophisticated that there is at
least one place in the world where each of them is considered "perverse."
But what finally convinces Mole of the rarity of joy and the prevalence
of pain among people, is the very next day, when he finally finds a use
for this handbook: it is so fragile, so thin, that he decides to use it to trim
his initial adolescent whiskers with; but then, on the very first stroke,
he cuts himself shaving.

Michael Benedikt, 1971

The Nipplewhip

Besides, what else could this be, this toothpick with the long eyelash attached to it with a spot of glue? And, oh, here come the fervent horsemen riding down from the shoulders now, in order to lift up the T-shirt or brassiere. Devils, torturers, these fiends know all too well that too much talk about the nipplewhip could some day cost the poet a fellowship! The poet and his/her love poems sink together into a gloom of handkissing. Meanwhile, at this very moment, all over that part of town with no taste, and no art, laughing people are flinging themselves directly into the path of the nipplewhip.

Michael Benedikt, 1976

Blasting from Heaven

> The little girl won't eat her sandwich;
> she lifts the bun and looks in, but the grey beef
> coated with relish is always there.
> Her mother says, "Do it for mother."
> Milk and relish and a hard bun that comes off
> like a hat—a kid's life is a cinch.
>
> And a mother's life? "What can you do
> with a man like that?" she asks the sleeping cook
> and then the old Negro who won't sit.
> "He's been out all night trying to get it.
> I hope he gets it. What did he ever do
> but get it?" The Negro doesn't look,
>
> though he looks like he's been out all night
> trying. Everyone's been out all night trying.
> Why else would we be drinking beer
> at attention? If she were younger,
> or if I were Prince Valiant, I would say that fate
> brought me here to quiet the crying,
>
> to sweeten the sandwich of the child,
> to waken the cook, to stop the Negro from
> bearing witness to the world. The dawn

still hasn't come, and now we hear
the 8 o'clock whistles blasting from heaven,
    and with no morning the day is sold.

Philip Levine, 1968

To a Child Trapped in a Barber Shop

You've gotten in through the transom
        and you can't get out
till Monday morning or, worse,
        till the cops come.

That six-year-old red face
        calling for mama
is yours; it won't help you
        because your case

is closed forever, hopeless.
        So don't drink
the Lucky Tiger, don't
        fill up on grease

because that makes it a lot worse,
        that makes it a crime
against property and the state
        and that costs time.

We've all been here before,
        we took our turn
under the electric storm
        of the vibrator

and stiffened our wills to meet
        the close clippers
and heard the true blade mowing
        back and forth

on a strip of dead skin,
        and we stopped crying.

You think your life is over?
      It's just begun.

Philip Levine, 1968

The Cemetery at Academy, California

On a hot summer Sunday
I came here with my children
who wandered among headstones
kicking up dust clouds. They found
a stone that said DAVI and
nothing more, and beneath the stone
a dead gopher, flat and dry.
Later they went off to play
on the dry dirt hills; I napped
under a great tree and woke
surprised by three teenagers.
They had put flowers in tin cans
around a headstone that showed
the sunrise over a slate sea,
and in the left-hand corner
a new bronze dove broke for peace.
Off in the distance my boys
had discovered the outhouses,
the twin white-washed sentinels,
and were unwinding toilet
paper and dropping whatever
they could find through the dark holes,
and when I found and scolded
them the two younger ones squeezed
my hands and walked stiffly at
my side past the three mourners.

I came here with a young girl
once who perched barefoot on her
family marker. "I will go
there," she said, "next to my sister."
It was early morning and
cold, and I wandered over
the pale clodded ground looking

for something rich or touching.
"It's all wildflowers in the spring,"
she had said, but in July
there were only the curled cut
flowers and the headstones blanked out
on the sun side, and the long
shadows deep as oil. I walked
to the sagging wire fence
that marked the margin of the
place and saw where the same ground,
festered here and there with reedy
grass, rose to a small knoll
and beyond where a windmill
held itself against the breeze.
I could hear her singing on
the stone under the great oak,
but when I got there she was
silent and I wasn't sure
and was ashamed to ask her,
ashamed that I had come here
where her people turned the earth.

Yet I came again, alone,
in the evening when the leaves
turned in the heat toward darkness
so late in coming. There was
her sister, there was her place
undisturbed, relatives and
friends, and other families
spread along the crests of this
burned hill. When I kneeled
to touch the ground it seemed like
something I had never seen,
the way the pale lumps broke down
to almost nothing, nothing
but the source of what they called
their living. She, younger now
than I, would be here some day
beneath the ground my hand combed.
The first night wind caught the leaves
above, crackling, and on

the trunk a salamander
faded in the fading light.
One comes for answers to a
place like this and finds even
in the darkness, even in
the sudden flooding of the
headlights, that in time one comes
to be a stranger to nothing.

Philip Levine, 1968

The Midget

In this café Durruti,
the unnamable, plotted
the burning of the Bishop
of Zaragoza, or so
the story goes. Now it's a hot
tourist spot in season, but
in mid-December the bar
is lined with factory workers
and day laborers as grey
as cement. The place smells
of cement and of urine,
and no one takes off his coat
or sits down to his sherry—
a queen's drink, as thin and dry
as benzine.
                It is Sunday,
late, and each man drinks alone,
seriously. Down the bar
a midget sings to himself,
sings of how from the starving South
he came, a boy, to this terrible
Barcelona, and ate. Not
all the songs are for himself;
he steps back from the bar,
his potbelly pushed out
and wrapped intricately
in a great, somber cummerbund,

and tells the world who is big,
big in the heart, and big down
here, big where it really counts.

Now he comes over to me,
and it is for me he sings.
Does he want money? I try
to buy him off with a drink,
a bored smile, but again
I hear of his power, of how
the Germans, Dutch, English—all
the world's babies—come to him,
and how on the fields of skin
he struts. "Here," he says to me,
"feel this and you'll believe."

In a voice suddenly thin
and adolescent, I tell him
I believe. "Feel this, feel this . . . "
I turn away from him, but
he turns with me, and the room
freezes except for us two.
I can smell the bitterness
of his sweat, and from the cracked
corners of his eyes see the tears
start down their worn courses.
I say, No, No more! He tugs
at my sleeve, hulking now, and
too big for his little feet;
he tugs and will not let go,
and the others along the bar
won't turn or interfere
or leave their drinks. He gets
my hand, first my forefinger
like a carrot in his fist,
and then with the other hand,
my wrist, and at last I can't
shake him off or defend myself.
            He sits in my lap
and sings of Americas,
of those who never returned

and those who never left. The smell
of anise has turned his breath
to a child's breath, but his cheeks,
stiff and peeling, have started
to die. They have turned along
the bar to behold me
on the raised throne of a torn
plastic barstool, blank and drunk
and half asleep. One by one
with the old curses thrown down
they pay up and go out,
and though the place is still
except for the new rumbling
of the morning catching fire
no one hears or no one cares
that I sing to this late-born freak
of the old world swelling my lap,
I sing lullaby, and sing.

Philip Levine, 1968

Baby Villon

He tells me in Bangkok he's robbed
Because he's white; in London because he's black;
In Barcelona, Jew; in Paris, Arab:
Everywhere and at all times, and he fights back.

He holds up seven thick little fingers
To show me he's rated seventh in the world,
And there's no passion in his voice, no anger
In the flat brown eyes flecked with blood.

He asks me to tell all I can remember
Of my father, his uncle; he talks of the war
In North Africa and what came after,
The loss of his father, the loss of his brother.

The windows of the bakery smashed and the fresh bread
Dusted with glass, the warm smell of rye

So strong he ate till his mouth filled with blood.
"Here they live, here they live and not die,"

And he points down at his black head ridged
With black kinks of hair. He touches my hair,
Tells me I should never disparage
The stiff bristles that guard the head of the fighter.

Sadly his fingers wander over my face,
And he says how fair I am, how smooth.
We stand to end this first and last visit.
Stiff, 116 pounds, five feet two,

No bigger than a girl, he holds my shoulders,
Kisses my lips, his eyes still open,
My imaginary brother, my cousin,
Myself made otherwise by all his pain.

Philip Levine, 1968

Animals are Passing from Our Lives

It's wonderful how I jog
on four honed-down ivory toes
my massive buttocks slipping
like oiled parts with each light step.

I'm to market. I can smell
the sour, grooved block, I can smell
the blade that opens the hole
and the pudgy white fingers

that shake out the intestines
like a hankie. In my dreams
the snouts drool on the marble,
suffering children, suffering flies,

suffering the consumers
who won't meet their steady eyes

for fear they could see. The boy
who drives me along believes

that any moment I'll fall
on my side and drum my toes
like a typewriter or squeal
and shit like a new housewife

discovering television,
or that I'll turn like a beast
cleverly to hook his teeth
with my teeth. No. Not this pig.

Philip Levine, 1968

A Kid on Her Way

The kid wanders, dazzled by the crowd
that buzzes in the mirrored plushy hall,
matrons, rapists, potheads: winners all.
The rhythm of the games, now hushed, now loud,
is the catching and slow loosing of the breath.
The tables beckon, pools of sequined hands:
beautiful, your face of light commands.
Deaf to the scarecrow mutter of varied death,
sure her fist of baubles will reverse
the turning drift of hungers, she makes her play.
The croupier rakes her brilliant chips away.
She rises, dazed, to fumble her light purse.
Draw a face on the mirror. Look hard. Blink twice.
A bit more death won't kill you. Try the dice.

Marge Piercy, 1968

Landed Fish

Danny dead of heart attack,
mid-forties, pretzel thin
just out of the pen for passing bad checks.
He made it as he could

and the world narrowed on him,
aluminum funnel of hot California sky.

In family my mother tells a story.
My uncle is sitting on the front steps,
it is late in the Depression,
my brother has dropped out of school.
Somehow today they got staked and the horses ran.
My uncle sits on the rickety front steps
under wisteria pale blue and littering scent.
I climb in his lap: I say
This is my Uncle Danny, I call him Donald for short,
oh how beautiful he is,
he has green eyes like my pussycat.
A Good Humor man comes jingling and Danny carries me
to buy a green popsicle on a stick,
first ice burning to sweet water on the tongue
in the long Depression
with cornmeal and potatoes and beans in the house to eat.

This story is told by my mother
to show how even at four I was cunning.
Danny's eyes were milky blue-green,
sea colors I had never known, verdigris, birdsheen.
The eyes of my cat were yellow. I was lying
but not for gain, mama. I squirm on his lap,
I am tangling my hands in his fiberglass hair.
The hook is that it pleases him
and that he is beautiful on the steps laughing
with money in the pockets of his desperate George Raft pants.
His eyes flicker like leaves,
his laugh breaks in his throat to pieces of sun.

Three years and he will be drafted and refuse to fight.
He will rot in stockade. He will swing an ax on his foot:
the total dropout who believed in his own luck.
I am still climbing into men's laps
and telling them how beautiful they are.
Green popsicles are still brief and wet and sweet.
Laughing, Danny leaves on the trolley with my brother.
He is feeling lucky, their luck is running
—like smelt, Danny—and is hustled clean

and comes home and will not eat boiled mush.
Late, late the wall by my bed shakes with yelling.

Fish, proud nosed conman, sea eyed tomcat:
you are salted away in the dry expensive California dirt
under a big neon sign shaped like a boomerang
that coaxes Last Chance   Stop Here   Last Chance.

Marge Piercy, 1968

The Death of the Small Commune

The death of the small commune
is almost accomplished.
I find it hard now to believe
in connection beyond the couple,
hard as broken bone.
Time for withdrawal and healing.
Time for lonely work
spun out of the torn gut.
Time for touching turned up earth,
for trickling seed from the palm,
thinning the shoots of green herb.
What we wanted to build
was a way station for journeying
to a new world,
but we could not agree long enough
to build the second wall,
could not love long enough
to move the heavy stone on stone,
not listen with patience
to make a good plan,
we could not agree.
Nothing remains but a shallow hole,
nothing remains
but a hole
in everything.

Marge Piercy, 1969

Learning Experience

The boy sits in the classroom
in Gary, in the United States, in NATO, in SEATO
in the thing-gorged belly of the sociobeast
in fluorescent light in slowly moving time
in boredom thick and greasy as vegetable shortening.
The classroom has green boards and ivory blinds,
the desks are new and the teachers not so old.
I have come out on the train from Chicago to talk
about dangling participles. I am supposed
to teach him to think a little on demand.
The time of tomorrow's draft exam is written on the board.
The boy yawns and does not want to be in the classroom in Gary
where the furnaces that consumed his father seethe rusty smoke
and pour cascades of nerve-bright steel
while the slag goes out in little dumpcars smoking,
but even less does he want to be in Today's Action Army
in Vietnam, in the Dominican Republic, in Guatemala,
in death that hurts.
In him are lectures on small groups, Jacksonian democracy,
French irregular verbs, the names of friends
around him in the classroom in Gary in the pillshaped afternoon
where tomorrow he will try and fail his license to live.

Marge Piercy, 1969

The Day the Perfect Speakers Left

It was as though it had begun to rain lightly
On the amazed stillness of birds
And leave-taking was another,
Sadder version of dusk we were attending,
And as though a whole age were going out,
Its head covered, and going out with it
A purpose including stars and stones.

What were their last words
Before the gates shut and small lights
Moved slowly up the hill of dark?

We were to mean everything this once,
Include in what we meant the birds and stars,
The stones too, and be no more watchers
On far shores, on single peaks, listeners
In little rooms, for news of how it is;
We were to hear the true last names for things,
The utter ode, composing us at last
In the rounding music of our sphere.

The gates are shut, the lights over the hill;
The barest voice softens in rain,
Streams out in wind, alleges more in dark than it knows.

Their words are hard to say, hard
To remember when you wake at dawn,
The bare light alerting you to plainness,
Solitude of stones, terror in birds,
Stars drifting off, the feel of huge leave-takings
For which no name, the first or last, consoles.
How can you trust those hints at dusk
Of foreign magnificence?

It may have all begun with a few native words,
Good, but made grandiose by wind or sad by rain,
Our own weather, sparing us a vaster silence.

This is when I turn, trusting you're here,
To say barely what's left, a few last words,
As though leave-taking itself composed
A plain majesty—the way light moved
So slowly up the hill of dark, who held
The light, his special purpose, the grief of gates,
What can't be said, but must. This is to leave
Almost without words, as though dumbfounding
The perfect speakers by including them also
In a fitting goodby.

And this is how stones are spoken for down here,
How birds, how stars, and the foreign mutterings
Of weather, and how men, and what they might mean.

Leonard Nathan, 1969

An Answer of Sorts

To Louis Simpson

Born to the suburbs,
Born to this wasteful middleclass life,
A neighbor sings in her small backyard,

As if she were in a procession
To the temple. She has simply forgotten herself
In the roses. Let her be. Let her be.

Leonard Nathan, 1969

The Suburb

No time, no time,
and with so many in line to be
born or fed or made love to, there is no
excuse for staring at it, though it's spring again
and the leaves have come out looking
limp and wet like little green new born babies.

The girls have come out in their new bought dresses,
carefully, carefully. They know they're in danger.
Already there are couples crumpled under the chestnuts.
The houses crowd closer, listening to each other's radios.
Weeds have got into the window boxes. The washing hangs,
helpless. Children are lusting for ice cream.

It is my lot each May to be hot and pregnant,
a long way away from the years when I slept by myself—
the white bed by the dressing table, pious with cherry blossoms,
the flatteries and punishments of photographs and mirrors.
We walked home by starlight and he touched my breasts.
"Please, please!" Then I let him anyway. Cars
droned and flashed, sucking at the cow parsley. Later
there were teas and the engagement party. The wedding
in the rain. The hotel where I slept in the bathroom.
The night when he slept on the floor.

The ache of remembering, bitter as a birth. Better
to lie still and let the babies run through me.
To let them possess me. They will spare me
spring after spring. Their hungers deliver me.
I grow fat as they devour me. I give them my sleep
and they absolve me from waking. Who can accuse me?
I am beyond blame.

Anne Stevenson, 1969

Apology

Mother, I have taken your boots,
your good black gloves, your coat
from the closet in the hall, your prettiest things.
But the way you disposed of your life gives me leave.
The way you gave it away.
Even as I pillage your bedroom,
make off with your expensive, wonderful books,
your voice streams after me, level with sensible urgency.
And near to the margin of tears as I used to be,
I do what you say.

Anne Stevenson, 1969

Dozing on the Porch with an Oriental Lap-rug

The aging pederast my friend
badgers me
to sign away my dead aunt's auctioned house
                        The screen goes black
The screen   I remember   I am awake on the sun porch
Chilly   and the tide is going out

Lotus blossoms   pears   the Indian ram
All the symbols   I can never remember what they mean
Every year the sea makes the rug forget
something of what it means

Whatever I was thinking whatever I was
dreaming about   nothing but dust and cinders
Old leaves

I let it go knowing only
it is four in the afternoon
a cold June so far
Cold enough for a fire

All day my head has been floating
above me
I am modest about it
What if one could would one sever
all connection with the body?
Favorite theory of mine
I am in love with my thinking

Slowly the weaving   the lotus blossoms
tide going out
snuffs out the borders   erases the screens

Richard Tillinghast, 1969

The Knife

For David Tillinghast

What was it I wonder?
   in my favorite weather   in the driving rain
      that drew me like a living hand
What was it
   like a living hand
that spun me off the freeway
      and stopped me
   on a sidestreet in California
with the rain pelting slick leaves down my windshield

to see the words of my brother's poem
      afloat on the bright air,
   and the knife I almost lost
      falling end over end through twenty years
         to the depths of Spring River—

the knife I had used to cut a fish open,
              caught in time
    the instant where it falls
              through a green flame of living water.

My one brother,
              who saw more in the river than water
    who understood what the fathers knew,
              dove from the Old Town canoe
        plunged and found his place
              in the unstoppable live water
seeing with opened eyes
              the green glow on the rocks
                    and the willows running underwater—
    like leaves over clear glass in the rain—

While the long-jawed, predatory fish
    the alligator gar
watched out of prehistory
        schooled in the water like shadows
              unmoved in the current,
    watched unwondering.

        The cold raw-boned, white-skinned boy
    curls off his dive in deep water
        and sees on the slab-rock
filling more space than the space it fills:

              the lost thing   *the knife*
    current swift all around it

and fishblood denser than our blood
    still stuck to the pike-jaw knifeblade
which carries a shape like the strife of brothers
                          —old as blood—
        the staghorn handle smooth as time.

    Now I call to him
              and now I see
    David burst into the upper air
gasping as he brings to the surface our grandfather's knife

shaped now, for as long as these words last,
    like all things saved from time.

I see in its steel
    the worn gold on my father's hand
        the light in those trees
the look on my son's face   a moment old

    like the river   old like rain
  older than anything that dies can be.

Richard Tillinghast, 1980

Our Flag Was Still There

For music, "Victory at Sea," or "In the Mood."

"Chessie," the Chesapeake and Ohio's
advertising mascot, snoozes
under sixty-mile-per-hour lamplight.
Two tabby kittens gaze saucer-eyed at their tomcat dad,
who sits alertly on his haunches,
soft fieldcap cocked to one side above neat,
pleasure-pursed lips and regimental whiskers.
One paw bandaged.
A Congressional Medal of Honor
red-white-and-blue-ribboned around his neck.
As convincingly at attention as a military-style,
family-oriented cat can be in a pullman car.
On his well-groomed chest, rows of campaign ribbons.
A dignified, "can do" look
hovers about his muscled smile.

In the luggage rack, a U.S. combat helmet
and a rising-sun flag in tatters.

I had a flag like that.
One of my three red-headed Marine cousins
brought it back from the South Pacific.
I thumbtacked it to the wall of my room.
The Japanese who had fought under it

perished in fierce firestorms.
They and their flag went up in that conflagration.

Our flag was still there.
Against a backdrop of blue sky and innocent clouds,
a line of six blunt-nosed P–47 fighters—
boxy and powerful like the grey Olds
we bought after the War
and drove to the Berkshires for the summer—
flew off on a mission to Corregidor.
The flag, unfurled in the stiff breeze,
was superimposed over the line of airplanes
on the cover of the Sunday magazine
one June morning in 1943.
The wind that made it wave as it does in pictures
blew off long ago toward Japan.

The sun nooned over orange groves and beaches.
Sparks from welding torches
illuminated the sleep of the City of the Angels
and darkened the sleep of others
as women workers beside the men
lowered masks over their faces,
and the children of New Jersey and Mississippi,
Europe and Detroit,
labored to make aluminum fly
and set afloat fleets of destroyers
and submarines radaring to the kill.

Looking ahead, there was a world of blue-grass lawns,
paneled wood enameled white, grandparents' faces
rosy over reassuring, hand-rubbed bannisters,
Yale locks, brass door-knockers, hardwood floors,
the odor of good furniture and wax,
a holiday design of holly leaves and berries on a stiff card,
a little girl holding gift packages as big as she is,
a boy, a real boy, bright as a new penny.

But now, in '43, the men and women pulled apart
like the elders of some stern, taboo-ridden tribe,
putting off till after the War the lives

of those who in twenty-five years
stood baffled on the 4th of July among uncles,
drove good German cars,
floated in tubs of hot, redwood-scented water with friends,
and greeted each other with the word, "Peace."

Richard Tillinghast, 1984

Second Decade

Let Not Your Hart Be Truble

For George Garrett

The horn of your silver bus
Sounds in the rocks and trees,
Black Saul of Tarsus turned Paul,
And you come telling
Under what tree and with what light
You were struck blind
And now see.

On faith and a curve, both blind,
You double-clutch and pass my car,
Hoping against the evidence
Of things not seen,
Or, should it appear from around this curve,
You trust the roadside rocks and trees
Will open like the sea.
That failing, you take the rock and wood
For what it gives.

Your pass is good, and made, I guess,
With the same thick hand that lettered
The words on your rear exit door:
LET NOT YOUR HART BE TRUBLE
You exact too much, black Paul,
My lane, my life on your faith,
My troubled hart.
And yet I do not deny you unlettered
The gift of metaphor, or even parable;
The master himself spoke thus,
Lest the heart of the many be softened.

You talk like you clutch, old black soul,
For you know the troubled hart
Takes the hunt
Into a deeper wood.

James Seay, 1970

Options

Rank on rank of false right eyes
Stared into my loss
And I saw
He would not find my soft brown eye,
Not in a thousand leather trays;
Not for all the purple velvet
That could be cut to lay them on
Was there an option
Able to resplit my sight
Or make me a king.
Not even his costly Orientals
Could fake my lost right eye.

He tried, eye after eye;
They lay like bogus coins
In my forehead.

Level with his window was a minaret
On whose globe he said
To fix my fluid left eye
For a truer fit.
As he ground with sand and steel
To shape blown glass to my blind side,
I saw again the world no longer turned
Around the sun,
Was flat, lacked depth,
Went neither beyond
Nor came before
The one-dimensional plane
Of sky and globe and minaret.

Into that vacancy
He placed the cold brown eye
My father paid him money for.
It was like a slug in the musicbox;
I could not play my song.
When I reached for things
They still were not there.

In the mirror beside his window
I tried again to find a true brown eye;

The truest there
Was in my father's saddened face.
Through the dark prosthetic glass
Vision came of my sovereign option:
I broke from his hand,
The stranger's vitreous smile, that humorless room,
And went into the park below.
Bell notes floated from the minaret
Like concentric waves in the fountain pool
Where I threw the mold-blown piece
And began to sort the planes,
Play the songs,
Between sky and globe and minaret,
Trusting depth to the patch of black
Behind my lost brown eye.

James Seay, 1970

The Ballet of Happiness

A letter comes from the city today
where she has just gone,
my student of a year ago,
to study art.
She says it is a long story
and asks among other things
if I am happy.

Instead of an answer of my own to send back,
I think of what she once gave
to the same question: she said no, not much,
but went on to name what in recent memory
had made her happy:

It was friends calling in the moonlight
to her balcony, saying they had come
to dance for her The Ballet of Happiness.
Which they did, their bright mescaline eyes
smiling up at her, and when it was over
they bowed like children in a play
and left—just walked across the grass,

leaving her dazzled and happy
with the funny shapes of their footwork
fading in the dew.

I have carried that dance a year in my head,
not realizing until now that for us too
friends appear on the damp lawn
and give us their blurred version
of a story they want to live
where image arises from image, freely,
and their kind bodies move for the words.

And we can be happy
because they have not come to take anything
but our smile
which we give in the freest of associations,
for they may never come again
or else forget and stay too long.

So am I happy?
It is a long story
and my feet are moving into moonlight
like clouds; friends are waiting.

James Seay, 1974

Homecoming

M. W. W., 1910–1964

I sit on my father's porch.
It is late. The evening, like
An old dog, circles the hills,
Anxious to settle. Across
Our road the fields and fruit trees,
Hedgerows and, out beyond, in
Another state, the misty
Approaches to the mountains,
Go quietly dark. In the
Close quarters of the yard white
Cape jasmine blossoms begin

To radiate light, become
Cold eyes. Into the sky the
Soft, loose Milky Way returns,
Gathering stars as it swarms
Deeper into the west. Now
Fireflies, like drops of blood, squirt
Onto the stiff leaves of the
Ivy vines, onto the bell
Lilies. Now I remember
Why I am here, and the sound
Of a breathing no longer
My own cuts through as I wait
For what must happen, for the
Flurry of wings, your dark claw.

Charles Wright, 1970

The New Poem

It will not resemble the sea.
It will not have dirt on its thick hands.
It will not be part of the weather.

It will not reveal its name.
It will not have dreams you can count on.
It will not be photogenic.

It will not attend our sorrow.
It will not console our children.
It will not be able to help us.

Charles Wright, 1973

Dog Creek Mainline

Dog Creek: cat track and bird splay,
Spindrift and windfall; woodrot;
Odor of muscadine, the blue creep
Of kingsnake and copperhead;

Nightweed; frog spit and floating heart,
Backwash and snag pool: Dog Creek

Starts in the leaf reach and shoal run of the blood;
Starts in the falling light just back
Of the fingertips; starts
Forever in the black throat
You ask redemption of, in wants
You waken to, the odd door:

Its sky, old empty valise,
Stands open, departure in mind; its three streets,
Y-shaped and brown,
Go up the hills like a fever;
Its houses link and deploy
—This ointment, false flesh in another color.

•

Five cutouts, five silhouettes
Against the American twilight; the year
Is 1941; remembered names
—Rosendale, Perry and Smith—
Rise like dust in the deaf air;
The tops spin, the poison swells in the arm:

The trees in their jade death-suits,
The birds with their opal feet,
Shimmer and weave on the shoreline;
The moths, like forget-me-nots, blow
Up from the earth, their wet teeth
Breaking the dark, the raw grain;

The lake in its cradle hums
The old songs: out of its ooze, their heads
Like tomahawks, the turtles ascend
And settle back, leaving their chill breath
In blisters along the bank;
Locked in their wide drawer, the pike lie still as knives.

•

Hard freight. It's hard freight
From Ducktown to Copper Hill, from Six

To Piled High: Dog Creek is on this line,
Indigent spur; cross-tie by cross-tie it takes
You back, the red wind
Caught at your neck like a prize:

(The heart is a hieroglyph;
The fingers, like praying mantises, poise
Over what they have once loved;
The ear, cold cave, is an absence,
Tapping its own thin wires;
The eye turns in on itself.

The tongue is a white water.
In its slick ceremonies the light
Gathers, and is refracted, and moves
Outward, over the lips,
Over the dry skin of the world.
The tongue is a white water.)

Charles Wright, 1973

Virgo Descending

Through the viridian (and black of the burnt match),
Through ox-blood and ochre, the ham-colored clay,
Through plate after plate, down
Where the worm and the mole will not go,
Through ore-seam and fire-seam,
My grandmother, senile and 89, crimpbacked, stands
Like a door ajar on her soft bed,
The open beams and bare studs of the hall
Pink as an infant's skin in the floating dark;
Shavings and curls swing down like snowflakes across her face.

My aunt and I walk past. As always, my father
Is planning rooms, dragging his lame leg,
Stroke-straightened and foreign, behind him,
An aberrant 2-by-4 he can't fit snug.
I lay my head on my aunt's shoulder, feeling
At home, and walk on.
Through arches and door jambs, the spidery wires

And coiled cables, the blueprint takes shape:
My mother's room to the left, the door closed;
My father's room to the left, the door closed—

Ahead, my brother's room, unfinished;
Behind, my sister's room, also unfinished.
Buttresses, winches, block-and-tackle: the scale of everything
Is enormous. We keep on walking. And pass
My aunt's room, almost complete, the curtains up,
The lamp and the medicine arranged
In their proper places, in arm's reach of where the bed will go . . .
The next one is mine, now more than half done,
Cloyed by the scent of jasmine,
White-gummed and anxious, their mouths sucking the air dry.

Home is what you lie in, or hang above, the house
Your father made, or keeps on making,
The dirt you moisten, the sap you push up and nourish . . .
I enter the living room, it, too, unfinished, its far wall
Not there, opening on to a radiance
I can't begin to imagine, a light
My father walks from, approaching me,
Dragging his right leg, rolling his plans into a perfect curl.
That light, he mutters, that damned light.
We can't keep it out. It keeps on filling your room.

Charles Wright, 1975

Rural Route

The stars come out to graze, wild-eyed in the new dark.
The dead squeeze close together,
Strung out like a seam of coal through the raw earth.
I smell its fragrance, I touch its velvet walls.

The willow lets down her hooks.
On the holly leaves, the smears of light
Retrench and repeat their alphabet,
That slow code. The boxwood leans out to take it on,

Quicker, but still unbroken.
Inside the house, in one room, a twelve-year-old

Looks at his face on the windowpane, a face
Once mine, the same twitch to the eye.

The willow flashes her hooks.
I step closer. Azalea branches and box snags
Drag at my pants leg, twenty-six years gone by.
I enter the wedge of light.

And the face stays on the window, the eyes unchanged.
It still looks in, still unaware of the willow, the boxwood
Or any light on any leaf. Or me.
Somewhere a tire squeals, somewhere a door is shut twice.

And what it sees is what it has always seen:
Stuffed birds on a desk top, a deer head
On the wall, and all the small things we used once
To push the twelve rings of the night back.

Charles Wright, 1975

Morandi

I'm talking about stillness, the hush
Of a porcelain center bowl, a tear vase, a jug.

I'm talking about space, which is one-sided,
Unanswered, and left to dry.

I'm talking about paint, about shape, about the void
These objects sentry for, and rise from.

I'm talking about sin, red drop, white drop,
Its warp and curve, which is blue.

I'm talking about bottles, and ruin,
And what we flash at the darkness, and what for . . .

Charles Wright, 1977

Snapshot

Under the great lens of heaven, caught
In the flash and gun of the full moon,
Improbable target in the lunar click,

My own ghost, a lock-shot lanyard of blue flame,
Slips from the deadeyes in nothing's rig,
Raiment and sustenance, and hangs

Like a noose in the night wind. Or like a mouth,
O-fire in the scaffolding. You are wine
In a glass, it says, you are sack, you are silt.

Charles Wright, 1977

Remembering San Zeno

After the end, they'll bring you
To someplace like this, columns of light propped through a west-facing
   door,
People standing about, echo of shoe-taps,
The gloom, like a grease-soaked rag, like a slipped skin
Left in a corner, puddled
In back of the votive stick stands, matter-of-factly—

Under the lisp and cold glow of the flames
Everything stares and moves closer, faces and blank hands,
October the 1st, 1975.
The banked candles the color of fresh bone,
Smoke rising from chimneys beyond the beyond,
Nightfires, your next address . . .

Charles Wright, 1977

Stone Canyon Nocturne

Ancient of Days, old friend, no one believes you'll come back.
No one believes in his own life anymore.

The moon, like a dead heart, cold and unstartable, hangs by a thread
At the earth's edge,
Unfaithful at last, splotching the ferns and the pink shrubs.

In the other world, children undo the knots in their tally strings.
They sing songs, and their fingers blear.

And here, where the swan hums in his socket, where bloodroot
And belladonna insist on our comforting,
Where the fox in the canyon wall empties our hands, ecstatic for more,

Like a bead of clear oil the Healer revolves through the night wind,
Part eye, part tear, unwilling to recognize us.

Charles Wright, 1977

from *Treasury Holiday*

I am the Gross National Product
absorb & including all things all goods Fab with Borax
Kleenex Clorox Kotex Kodak & Ex-Lax
I contain the spectacular car-crash death of the movie star
         Jayne Mansfield
& the quiet death of John Masefield the word star equally
the Baby Ruth no less than the Crab Nebula
I do not distinguish or discriminate the murmuring
of pine & poison The gross the great the grand National
pure products the good doc said go crazy
Lord God of Hosts I am the Gross National Product of the
         United States of America & here celebrate the New Fiscal Year
this fourth of July in the Lord's anno
one thousand plus one thousand minus one hundred plus fifty
         plus ten plus five plus three ones
in Mod. Am. Eng. ALFA DELTA 11110110000
I am the grand central Brother Jonathan & Uncle Sam
red white & blue-black all

I am first second & third persons singular & plural nominative
    genitive accusative & focative
absorbing & subsuming all including Mister Fats Domino
Alexander Hamilton the handsome treasurer & Gaylord Wilshire
    & Sylvester Graham & Mary Baker Eddy
O national product composed of compositions of all sorts of sorts
melting pot mulligan mulligatawny & huge buildings
& I reject the government as such for the government as nonesuch
& I categorically deny education religion youth communication love
    industry poetry & all arts & sciences & games & nature & culture
all subordinated quite to one gross & national product in terms of
the lordly Long Green
money the only mother
money the only poetry
they say LSD in England pounds shillings pence O pounds of money
money the only gross national poem & noumenon
for it is a good thing to me including all things & by its intermediation
    making them all holy one & all
the cheap ugly vulgar things
& language
holy body of money the only poetry
O gross & National bills coins post stamps lard futures bonds
    vouchers gilt-edge blue-chip shares checks & military payment
    certificates & rapid-transit tokens

William Harmon, 1970

from *Legion: Civic Choruses*

The Ceremon(y)(ies) of Mutability

the road to hell is paved with theologians.
the golden gates are hanging on their hinges weeping.

an orphaned wildebeest stares at the ruined altar rinsed in the
    Sunday-funny Dutch reformed light.
a hundred thousand hungover white candles hear an ah.

wicked dirt from pterodactyls drops like preternature's dumb bombs
    'pon the candy-paper mobile homes of us posthistoric men.

Papists & Maoists.
kleagles & kleavers & Amos & Remus & old Adam Bum.

they speak in tongues from limb to limb.

William Harmon, 1973

Invoice No. 13
A Masque of Resignation

I bought a pack of Camels yesterday.
What do I care if World War III breaks out?
Whatever happens happens anyway.

Not gold, not bronze, not dust itself can stay.
Nothing at all endures, not even doubt.
I bought a pack of Camels yesterday.

Today there grows a bay tree by the bay.
Tomorrow both bays will die in a drought.
Whatever happens happens anyway.

The sun will rise, will shine, and—come what may—
Will set. I don't know what it's all about.
I bought a pack of Camels yesterday.

Say what you like. Can I care what you say?
If you aspire to sainthood, be devout.
Whatever happens happens anyway.

I drive an eighteen-year-old Chevrolet.
You, optimist, can let me be a lout.
I bought a pack of Camels yesterday;
Whatever happens happens anyway.

William Harmon, 1985

Swallow the Lake

Gave me things I
could not use. Then. Now.
Rain night bursting upon & into. I
shine updown into Lake Michigan

like the glow from the cold lights of the Loop.
Walks. Deaths. Births.
Streets. Things I could not give back. Nor
use. Or night or day or night or

loneliness. Other ways   feelings I could not
put into words   into themselves into people.
Blank monkeys of the hierarchy. More deaths—
stupidity & death turning them on

into the beat of my droopy heart   my middle
passage blues my corroding hate my release
while I come to become neon iron eyes stainless lungs
blood zincgripped steel I
come up abstract

not able to take their bricks. Tar. Nor their flesh.
I ran: stung. Loop fumes hung
                              in my smoky lungs.

Ideas I could not break nor form. Gave me
things I
see break & run down the crawling down the game.

Illusion illusion, and you
would swear before screaming somehow
choked voices in me.

The crawling thing in the blood, the
huge immune loneliness. One becomes immune
to the bricks the feelings. One becomes
death.
One becomes each one and every person I
become. I could not
I COULD NOT

I could not whistle and walk in storms
along Lake Michigan's shore. Concrete walks.
I could not swallow the lake.

Clarence Major, 1970

My Seasonal Body, My Ears

6 months I was in
the ratio of the weight of myself,
in myself calm sad by volume

substance and volume. Some kind
of soldier who could not clean the
lonely hospital hall from

the spirit of my one hundred
& fifty pounds, with light finding
the regular shapes out of the strange

natural chestful of sour oranges I
remember each elastic moment
of each grave space of my solitary cold

stay. Warm locality the sky, boats or sea
out so heavy, lonesome far to land stood
then the perfect rotunda of all the time

left in me, 16 years old: the holes fragments
in my head, eyes so desolate, the weight
of myself so young so yearning

Clarence Major, 1970

Suburban

What ought to be admired, then? Not the children, surely,
who are undisciplined energies, smashing their tricycles
into each other, screaming like machinery screaming.

And not the mothers, spreadeagled on the porch steps
discussing Crisco and the social status of policemen,
the huge rollers of their hair bobbing above their chat.

Nor the two together, for the mothers alternately
like pop-up toasters cry warnings, "Don't do that!"
and then relapse, while the children do and do.

Off somewhere in night's perimeters, the fathers
fidget with their flies. Can they call themselves at once
fiercely masculine and yet easily understanding?

No one can tell, no one having seen them since
the last surgery of begetting. They have paid in their time
at the bowling alley, have guiltily given blood.

Around stand, range on range, the mixed frontiers
of the architecture, a wilderness crossed by nomads
on thin caravan routes that lead to the real cities,

and the genius of the place, the aborigine
is the woman in the next apartment who hates her son
and says everything twice. "I'll stew him." Pause. "I'll stew him."

What ought to be admired? The vague sea fog
obscuring the precision of the planted palms?
The wind, harrowing up the brief grass clippings?

William Dickey, 1971

So full of sleep are those who lose the way
that they wander, under the bent eaves of the night
into the shadow only of a spectral moonlight
that seems to them more enduring than the day.

So full of darkness that the natural sun
is to their eyes an injury, a fierce stone.
They cannot keep themselves safely their own
under the inquiries of that broad noon

and so will seek the entry underground,
the unmoved shore, the silent and unmoved water,

where the echo of speech is thinned, the echo of laughter
turns to a thread of vacancy, no sound.

Until even the memory of the shape of day
is less than shadow to them, and their breath
dreams through their nostrils the transparent death
that, full of sleep, now leads them on their way.

William Dickey, 1971

The Floor

For Charles Simic

The floor is something we must fight against. Whilst seemingly
mere platform for the human stance, it is that place that men fall to.

I am not dizzy. I stand as a tower, a lighthouse; the pale ray of my
sentiency flowing from my face.
But should I go dizzy I crash down into the floor; my face into the
floor, my attention bleeding into the cracks of the floor.

Dear horizontal place, I do not wish to be a rug. Do not pull at the
difficult head, this teetering bulb of dread and dream. . . .

Russell Edson, 1973

Lovers

There was a blind owl which was loved by a squirrel with a crushed
head.
If the squirrel thought the owl was a squirrel, the owl thought the
squirrel was an owl—Did it matter?—I mean, in the night, would it mat-
ter when the squirrel was upon its mate; the owl on her back pressing
closer the squirrel with wings dormant for love . . .
And could it matter after the act when the great woman owl mur-
mured, don't move, stay . . .
The squirrel is restless.
The owl sighing, don't move, honey . . .

The squirrel wants a drink of water, I'll be back in a minute . . .
Stay with me, honey . . .

Many nights of this.

Russell Edson, 1973

The Large Thing

A large thing comes in.
Go out, Large Thing, says someone.
The Large Thing goes out, and comes in again.
Go out, Large Thing, and stay out, says someone.
The Large Thing goes out, and stays out.
Then that same someone who has been ordering the Large
Thing out begins to be lonely, and says, come in, Large Thing.
But when the Large Thing is in, that same someone decides it would
be better if the Large Thing would go out.
Go out, Large Thing, says this same someone.
The Large Thing goes out.
Oh, why did I say that? says the someone, who begins to
be lonely again.
But meanwhile the Large Thing has come back in anyway.
Good, I was just about to call you back, says the same
someone to the Large Thing.

Russell Edson, 1976

The Tearing and Merging of Clouds . . .

. . . So it is given: we follow as through a tunnel down through
the trees into the earth, where the dead swim cleansed of the world;
innocent in undiscovered desire . . .
Chains of events hold between points, bridges that are not for the
traveler, but for the seer, for whom such bridges are unnecessary . . .
The porridge on the table longs for the ceiling, dreaming of new
plasticities . . .
The window watches with all its meadows and rivers, its trees lean-
ing in the wind to see more fully . . .
Everything is made of time, and we go out in waves, accumulating

around ourselves in halos of dust; the borders bleeding each into the other; the tearing and merging of clouds . . .

Russell Edson, 1976

The Way Things Are

There was a man who had too many mustaches. It began with the one on his upper lip, which he called his normal one.

He would say, this is my normal mustache.

But then he would take out another mustache and put it over his real mustache, saying, this is my abnormal one.

Then he would take out another mustache and put it over the other two and say, this one's normal.

And then another over the other three, saying, this one's abnormal.

And after several more layers he was asked why he wanted to have so many normal and abnormal mustaches.

He said, it's not that I want to, it's simply the way things are . . .

Then he took all the mustaches off. They like a rest, he murmured.

The first mustache, which we thought was real, was not.

We mentioned to him that we thought his first mustache was real.

He said, it is, all my mustaches are real; it's just that some of them are normal, and some of them are abnormal; it's simply the way things are . . .

Russell Edson, 1985

The Rat's Legs

I met a rat under a bridge. And we sat there in the mud discussing the rat's loveliness.

I asked, what is it about you that has caused men to write odes?

My legs, said the rat, for it has always been that men have liked to run their hands up my legs to my secret parts; it's nature . . .

Russell Edson, 1985

My Grandmother Had Bones

My grandmother had bones as delicate
As ivory umbrella ribs. Orphaned
Early, she craved things no one could give her.
She boiled kettles dry and threw in her hand
If she was losing. No one outlived her.
But her health was never quite good. Her cat
Killed birds and made her cry. Still she kept him.
She loved green tea, postcards, things from far off.
'Where does the time go to?' she would sigh.
She went to bed, to mass, coughed her little cough.
She braided my hair like honey, but I
Had Mother to do it over tight. Some whim
Made her dislike me, but I didn't care,
I thought. Why then, when she died, did I dream
She was a package of frozen meat?
Why was I chosen to throw her in the stream?
Why, when I had the bundle gathered neat
Did her raw wristbone scrape against my hair?

Judith Hemschemeyer, 1973

Giving Birth in Greek

Giving birth in Greek
only took two words.

The midwife smoothed my hair,
coaxed my legs into stirrups
and gave me the shot

that sent my head
high into a corner
of that dazzling room

from where I watched it all.

There was a wild animal
stuck inside me,
struggling to get out

and I could see
I was doing everything I could
to help it:

breathing evenly,
exhaling at the crest
of the contractions

not pushing

still not pushing

giving those muscles,
those raw, stubborn snails,
one last chance to break my back

and mold me into whatever shape
it needed to escape.

Then all at once
it was that moment
when I knew if I pushed
I would die

and if I didn't push
I would die
but it would still be inside me

and 'Tora!' 'Now!' she shouted

and we both bore down
and the beast became my son
and slid into her hands.

'Oraia,' 'Beautiful,'
she said. 'Oraia.'

Later, in my room, in the dark,
I started to bleed a lot
and I knew I should call the nurse

but I didn't know the words.

Anyway there were no more words.

I lay all night
in that cold, clotting stain,
wide open, wide awake

and falling in love
all over again.

Judith Hemschemeyer, 1975

Margaret Whiting Tearfully Sings

Then there were those days on lower Broadway
using just enough to keep a room at the
University Hotel so you could sit at the window
in your lime green underwear hoping for some business
or at least a pure shot
for old times sake
all I could do
was sit on the toilet and drool into a paper cup
asking you to drink milk
to go to sleep to
please
get dressed or get undressed completely
Instead
you brought the radio into the bathroom
touching my hair while I cried over Margaret Whiting singing
'Moonlight in Vermont'   one more time one more
time

where are you
where are all your friends whose taste ran to
imitation red leather and see through blouses that kept me
weeping on the toilet for days on end
I still worry about the people I didn't make love to
were their grandmothers ever cured, did they

earn enough money
did someone find them in time

Eleanor Lerman, 1973

Evenings in the Sea

I feel such people making love behind old stairways
crooning wordless syllables to themselves
In burned out armories they lay themselves down
      in charred brick
rocking back and forth in arms that touch and linger
as much on one skin as on the other
On evenings born of a blue mood I feel them in the sea
turning the color of old suns as they
drift across the meridians,
men who cannot remember what a man is
and women, releasing fingernails and hair
turning forever back to a lover they do not
chastise or name
In the middle of the day I feel people disappearing quietly
in pairs, forgetting form and gender,
slipping deep into the sky
with whoever sat beside them on the train
or had the right time on the way to work
In my mind I am everyone,
needing you if only to have something of myself
Close your eyes and forget me,
tell me what you regret
and we will go on

Eleanor Lerman, 1973

Gabriel's Blues

Everyone's going to ride tomorrow
Though poor sons lie, steal; I know
The air of Jesus: whirling strongly,

Becoming a wall. Come to my comfort
Child and hear the horses in my head.
On the road read their direction; one

Ear lies unwounded: listen to the hoofs
From the other side of the world explode.
I know days when altars open like a mouth

Stretching out for air and sounds breaking
Become a shield bright below me while his
Dust and dirt blow into my trailing face.

Calvin Forbes, 1974

My Father's House

1908–1970

I live quietly and go nowhere
And this house shakes like a tree.
Open the door, Jesus is the hinge
Squeaking from the rusty rain.

Deadheart, this house wasn't built
By human hands, and no bricks will
You find, wood or glass. This house
Stands like a skeleton inside the worst

Possible skin. Knock and enter afraid,
Your shadow rigid as the brass laid
Across your coffin. Come closer and see
Broken beams, a sacred slum, no mystery

Except memory. Rise and make ends meet
My tenant. Safe in its vastness, retreat
To a hidden corner; without mercy guard
Its secret life as if a fortune were yours.

Calvin Forbes, 1974

Mother, R.I.P.

When our dead mother came back on the tenth
anniversary of her death, wearing
a floor-length flowered shift with a straw hat
over the wiglet and the bottled tan,
we all assured her that she hadn't aged
a day, that she had lost some weight, that she
had gained a worldliness which often comes
with travel. What we felt in secret was
how smug she seemed, considering the tears
we'd spent on her behalf and all those mums
we'd planted at her grave. She poured the tea
like Lady Astor at the Orphan's Home
—*Another lump of sugar dear?*—while we,
wanting to squeeze her hand, wanting to sing
or rage, wanting to tell her every day's
adventures, every year's meanderings,
sat at her feet like stone. Said nothing true.
Said *Bless you mother* when she stood to leave
and never learned, and never thought to ask,
where she had been, what she was heading toward.

Barbara L. Greenberg, 1974

A Midnight Diner by Edward Hopper

Your own greyhounds bark at your side.
It is you, dressed like a Sienese,
Galloping, ripping the gown as the fabled
White-skinned woman runs, seeking freedom.
Tiny points of birches rise from hills,
Spin like serrulate corkscrews toward the sky.
In other rooms it is your happiness
Flower petals fall for, your brocade
You rediscover, feel bloom upon your shoulder.

And freedom's what the gallery's for.
You roam in large rooms and choose your beauty.
Yet, Madman, it's your own life you turn back to:
In one postcard purchase you wipe out

Centuries of light and smiles, golden skin
And openness, forest babes and calves;
You forsake the sparkler breast
That makes the galaxies; you betray
The women who dance upon the water

All for some bizarre hometown necessity!
Some ache still found within you!
Now it will go with you, this scene
By Edward Hopper and nothing else.
It will become your own tableau of sadness
Composed of blue and grey already there.
Over or not, this suffering will not say Hosanna.
Now a music will not come out of it.
Grey hat, blue suit, you are in a midnight
Diner painted by Edward Hopper.

Here is a man trapped at midnight underneath the El.
He's sought the smoothest counter in the world
And found it here in the almost empty street,
Away from everything he has ever said.
Now he has the silence they've insisted on.
Not a squirrel, not an autumn birch,
Not a hound at his side, moves to help him now.
His grief is what he'll try to hold in check.
His thumb has found and held his coffee cup.

David Ray, 1974

On the Photograph "Yarn Mill," by Lewis W. Hine

A boy, age about eleven,
looking just like my son Sam—
same flaxen hair, same cap
I gave him—long-sleeve
shirt tucked in overalls,
standing between iron spinning
mules in a yarn mill, his dirty
right hand touching the machine,
which is huge and black like oil
and no doubt clacking away, stamped

"MASON MACHINE WORKS
PATENT MASS 1903" in a circle
around a nub, like the other,
so that he is caught between
those two great breasts of iron.
His left hand hangs free
and we could still reach out
and pull him safe unto us. Spools
of yarn recede down rows
beyond him as in the mirrors
of a barbershop; the humming
strings look like the innards
of long pianos whose music dins;
the yarn is beaten now by wooden
mallets, then woven—sheared,
combed, dyed—whatever
the boss men say, in North Carolina,
1908. The boy's face, like Sam's,
is trusting, gazes almost amused
at what's before him. This year,
luckily, a horse. Not a yarn
mill. In a dream last night
I watched my son assemble
the temple of his life as from
a kit (he was named for kings)
and now I see him standing
between those steel machines,
a boy who had no temple,
who could reach out and touch
that cold iron breast,
then knock it off to joke with men.

David Ray, 1987

This Is a Sad-Ass Poem for a Black Woman to Be Writing

We have not, up to
now, known each other.
The light jive and fly
speech over public

tables do not count
for much.
        I look for
you at your place, in
the few books and bare
walls, even listen
for echoes of you
in the music. I no-
tice an old milk car-
ton; I hear so much
anonymous noise.

You expend yourself—
something—within me
and I pant beneath
you, open, heaving.
You withdraw; I close
and stillness and breath,
bodies burrowing
into damp sheets are
the only sounds in
the silence. Silence:

Good jive, a light rap
and fly speech over
a public table.

Sherley Williams, 1975

Quartet

I
I piece together my child
hood for my son and this is
more than reminiscence more
than who said or what happened
or what I have done. I weave
the word ritual where time
and pace are meaning, weave it
best in anger and love: You

don't be*lieve* fat-meat greasy,
huh? as I wield the belt; grunt
behind his good night kiss, say
yo suga almos mo'n one
mamma can stand; giving him
sounds to link what's gone with what
we renew in our coming.

II
If you have to tell someone
the answer, the question might
as well have been left unsaid.
There's no one answer; old or
new, the form the answer gives
itself can take you home and
even walking with strangers
is like being with people
you've always known.
                            I can
say the word is Thunderbird
even recall the price, tell
of wooden gods and what God
love; that's what my mamma told
me. Her rhythm, her tone—now
mine—were keys to Shine whom I
knew before I was ten, to
the monkey signifying
in the trees but I didn't learn
about them at mamma's knee.

III
I thought—he said—like Lit, I
tease a kid's remark that ought
to crack him up (Yet where would
he have heard it?) Who's Lit he
asks and sorry now I said
it, shrug and smile. Oh some
ol rhyme we played when I was
young and call to him to watch
for cars as he starts across
the street. Lit, writ, spit, he chants.

The chant floats back to me,
reminder of what I can
and can't give him: While mammas
can talk that Lit-talk to you—
definitely will do it—
you bet'not even *think* Lit
in front of them. And telling
him just that much would blow it.

IV
In a conference room—this
is from a long time ago—
among white and almost white
professionals I capped with
Lit to end discussion and
a brotha responded with
a grin. We laughed like crazy
and though no one else under
stood the joke they knew that in
our laugh the brotha and I
gather and speak as one tongue.

Sherley Williams, 1975

For Ronald King Our Brother

whom we love, whose actions
are rooted in our common rage
and whose pain we were powerless
to ease, this poem for the present.

It cannot recall the explosion or
quicken the earth bound body
or make any single past present
to be changed or lived again.

Poems are crafted thought, channelled feeling
and now . . . Now. Yes, and living
set in one moment of timeless

time   always and love.   Love.
We hope it is not too late:

                              We rock you
in the cradle of our soul.

Sherley Williams, 1975

The Lost Pilot

For my father, 1922–1944

Your face did not rot
like the others—the co-pilot,
for example, I saw him

yesterday. His face is corn-
mush: his wife and daughter,
the poor ignorant people, stare

as if he will compose soon.
He was more wronged than Job.
But your face did not rot

like the others—it grew dark,
and hard like ebony;
the features progressed in their

distinction. If I could cajole
you to come back for an evening,
down from your compulsive

orbiting, I would touch you,
read your face as Dallas,
your hoodlum gunner, now,

with the blistered eyes, reads
his braille editions. I would
touch your face as a disinterested

scholar touches an original page.
However frightening, I would
discover you, and I would not

turn you in; I would not make
you face your wife, or Dallas,
or the co-pilot, Jim. You

could return to your crazy
orbiting, and I would not try
to fully understand what

it means to you. All I know
is this: when I see you,
as I have seen you at least

once every year of my life,
spin across the wilds of the sky
like a tiny, African god,

I feel dead. I feel as if I were
the residue of a stranger's life,
that I should pursue you.

My head cocked toward the sky,
I cannot get off the ground,
and, you, passing over again,

fast, perfect, and unwilling
to tell me that you are doing
well, or that it was mistake

that placed you in that world,
and me in this; or that misfortune
placed these worlds in us.

James Tate, 1967

A Guide to the Stone Age

For Charles Simic

A heart that resembles a cave,
a throat of shavings,
an arm with no end and no beginning:

How about the telephone?
—Not yet.

The cave in your skull,
a throat with a crack in it,
a heart that still resembles a cave:

How about the knife?
—Later.

The fire in the cave of your skull,
a beast who died shaving,
a cave with no end and no beginning:

A big ship!
—Shut up.

Instructions which ask you to burn other instructions,
a circle with a crack in it,
a stone with an arm:

A hat?
—Not the hat.

A ship with a knife in it,
a telephone with a hat over it,
a cave with a heart:

The Stone Age?
—There's no end to it.

James Tate, 1972

A Dime Found in the Snow

Tomorrow the future will be here,
open her great droopy eye.
She will clean out the barn
with a white boa thrown round her neck
while the pterodactyl dreams
in his floral chambers, destitute
of feathers and the supporting surface
of wings, dreams of the difference
between a long time and a short time,
of getting out of this life
and staying—a flower and a fire engine,
out of this world. Miss Future
might remember something, some summer,

but she's tired and anxious
for a new oblivion, something
to agitate her. Just for the hell of it
she has the ball on the lawn
roll away from home. The opponent,
her father, takes advantage of this
situation, this holiday, and pours
a flame through her yawning hoop,
a red nothing, one of everything.
And, with spite for tomorrow's sameness,
makes the wild river quiet inside.
With all her sex she turns away
from this possible unnatural temple

of transmogrified instants,
and throws a few gravestones
at her children, asleep in manicured
detachment, in an airplane that floats
like a song, in a Cadillac full
of roses (that stalls on the beach),
and on seahorses that back
into their twinkling caves;
an inclination to cling to them,
to not let them slip, to let them sleep—
an icicle that grows from a tree,

a feather thrown into a canyon,
a dime found in the snow.

James Tate, 1976

Goodtime Jesus

Jesus got up one day a little later than usual. He had been dreaming so
deep there was nothing left in his head. What was it? A nightmare, dead
bodies walking all around him, eyes rolled back, skin falling off. But he
wasn't afraid of that. It was a beautiful day. How 'bout some coffee?
Don't mind if I do. Take a little ride on my donkey, I love that donkey.
Hell, I love everybody.

James Tate, 1979

Land of Little Sticks, 1945

Where the wife is scouring the frying pan
and the husband is leaning up against the barn.
Where the boychild is pumping water into a bucket
and the girl is chasing a spotted dog.

And the sky churns on the horizon.
A town by the name of Pleasantville has disappeared.
And now the horses begin to shift and whinny,
and the chickens roost, keep looking this way and that.
At this moment something is not quite right.

The boy trundles through the kitchen, spilling water.
His mother removes several pies from the oven, shouts at him.
The girlchild sits down by the fence to stare at the horses.
And the man is just as he was, eyes closed, forehead
against his forearm, leaning up against the barn.

James Tate, 1983

Storm

The snow visits us,
taking little bits of us with it,
to become part of the earth,
an early death and an early return—

like the filing of tax forms.
And all you can say after adding up
column after column: "I'm not myself."

And all you can say after the long night
of searching for one certain scrap of paper:
"It never existed."

And when all the lamps are lit
and the smell of the stew
has followed you upstairs
and slipped under the door of your study:
"The lute is telling the story
of the life I might have lived,
had I not—"

In my study, which is without heat,
in mid-January, in the hills
of a northern province—only
the thin white-haired volumes
of poetry speak, quietly, like
unfed birds on a night visit

to a cat farm. And an airplane is lost
in a storm of fitting pins.
The snow falls, far into the interior.

James Tate, 1986

Consolations After an Affair

My plants are whispering to one another:
they are planning a little party

later on in the week about watering time.
I have quilts on beds and walls
that think it is still the 19th century.
They know nothing of automobiles and jet planes.
For them a wheat field in January
is their mother and enough.
I've discovered that I don't need
a retirement plan, a plan to succeed.
A snow leopard sleeps beside me
like a slow, warm breeze.
And I can hear the inner birds singing
alone in this house I love.

James Tate, 1990

Tropics

In the still morning when you move
toward me in sleep for love,
I dream of

an island where long-stemmed cranes,
serious weather vanes,
turn slowly on one

foot. There the dragonfly folds
his mica wings and rides
the tall reed

close as a handle. The hippo yawns,
nods to thick pythons,
slack and drowsy, who droop down

like untied sashes
from the trees. The brash
hyenas do not cackle

and run but lie with their paws
on their heads like dogs.
The lazy crow's caw

falls like a sigh. In the field
below, the fat moles build
their dull passage with an old

instinct that needs
no light or waking; its slow beat
turns the hand in sleep

as we turn toward each other
in the ripe air of summer,
before the change of weather,

before the heavy drop
of the apples.

Ellen Bryant Voigt, 1976

At the Edge of Winter

Vacant cornstalks rattle in the field,
the ditches are clogged with wet leaves.
Under the balding maple, toadstools
cluster like villages; their ruffled
undersides are brown. Inside,
we prepare for children: the clean
linens, the perfumed loins,
the aphrodisiac are ready. The cat,
our pagan daughter, has brought
her offering—the half-eaten, headless
carcass of a rabbit; its bright guts
bloom on the back porch step.

Rich November! Under the stiff
brown grass, the earth's maw
is full of tulip bulbs, hyacinth
and crocus to mull and ripen
these long months in deep freeze.
This is our season of opulence.
Festive, extravagant,

we'll spend your creamy seed
like the feathered milkweed blowing open.

Smeared with rabbit blood like a pagan,
I hack down the last new shoots
of the rosebush and arrange a bed
of rose and red cedar to scent
the fertile wound of the rabbit, lying
open and ready, primed for the winding
sheet of snow and the restless track
of the gray creative worm.

Ellen Bryant Voigt, 1976

Claiming Kin

Insistent as a whistle, her voice up
the stairs pried open the blanket's
tight lid and piped me
down to the pressure cooker's steam and rattle.
In my mother's kitchen, the hot iron spit
on signal, the vacuum cleaner whined
and snuffled. Bright face
and a snazzy apron, clicking her long spoons,
how she commandeered the razzle-dazzle!

In the front room I dabbed
the company chairs with a sullen rag.
Pale lump blinking at the light,
I could hear her sing in her shiny kingdom,
the sound drifted out like a bottled message.
It was the voice of a young girl,
who stopped to gather cool moss,
forgetting the errand, spilling the cornmeal,
and cried and cried in her bearish papa's ear.

At night, while I flopped like a fish
on grandma's spool bed, up from her bed
and my wheezing father she rose to the holly,

flat-leaf and Virginia Creeper.
Soft ghost, plush as a pillow,
she wove and fruited against the black hours:
red berries and running cedar, green signatures
on the table, on the mantel.

Mother, this poem is from your middle
child who, like your private second self
rising at night to wander the dark house,
grew in the shady places:
a green plant in a brass pot,
rootbound, without blossoms.

Ellen Bryant Voigt, 1976

The Heart is the Target

For Louise

Hunger drove you across
the savannah and into the rainy
forest, sweating for prey.
As if this heat were an ally;
as if desire were a weapon.

Now you have reached the densest
vegetation. The path behind you
has closed like a curtain of water.
You have come upwind of your quarry.
The birds, with their passionate
language, announce your arrival.

Flushed by the chase, you lounge
on a viny cushion. Above the belly's
salt-lick, your breasts thrust forward
their wine-soaked centers. You strip
to the waist—a wash of light
against the green canvas. Soon,

in a murmur of branches, a figure
approaches. He sights the white field,
aims for the left breast's two

concentric circles. Then the pull
of the dark, centripetal eye.

Ellen Bryant Voigt, 1976

The Visit

The afternoon spreads its fingers on the lawn,
and such light as penetrates the shrubs
enters the house with hesitation.
I have come from a great distance
to find my father asleep in his large brown chair.
Why isn't he out in the fields, our common passion?
I want to wake him with kisses,
I want to reach out and stroke his hand.
But I turn away, without speech or gesture,
having for so long withheld my body from him.

Ellen Bryant Voigt, 1976

Ukrainian Pastoral

From a photo of my grandparents

On a wooded hillside by a river, a woman pauses
To catch her breath, leans against a silver birch.
What she sees we can't know, for her eyes are shut.
She is stocky, young; her calves glisten in sunlight.
When she opens her eyes to admit us, the earth
Is a maypole around which she sweeps a clearing.

Upon the water, a small boat is making its way
Toward shore, a man rowing, his muscular shoulders
Propelling him through mist. Perhaps he envisions
This shape on the hillside, who might be a wife
Or a sweetheart, waiting. But his back is to us.
Perhaps he shuts his eyes to hear the river's pulse.

When I enter the parlor, I think you've been reading
The book on your lap, but your eyes are shut.

I remove my old coat. I see a parakeet preening
In its cage, and a salad of onion and cucumber
Set on a table by a vase of yellow iris.
Was it something you heard, my foot on the walk,

That woke you? Or does light convert us into people,
Husband and wife, the one reading, the other
Entering an arch as he does each day of his life?
On the wall, a woman partially hidden by trees,
And a man gliding over water, about whom we can
Invent a story, or better, say nothing and wait.

Steve Orlen, 1978

The Biplane

For Rolly Kent

Sometimes the night is not enough. I rise remembering,
And the dream is no longer a quaint story
In another's life, but my own grown more real.
Last night a biplane landed in my neighbor's field.
I watched, from my window seat, the canvas wings
Graze the rows of corn and come to rest.
                                        Afternoons
Seem always time between the crests of dream. There is
An oak outside my window so stunted, its limbs
Elbowing this way and that, it seems it had made
A decision not to grow beyond its needs. In spring
The leaves appear, in fall they yellow and curl,
And I know the constant change in direction is a
Ruse to make it seem more humble.
                                        Again last night
The biplane landed in my neighbor's field.
It caught fire, but when the wind finally blew
It out, I felt like the child who snuffs a match
In a closet and finds himself alone and bodiless.
Just think: I forgot the dream today. I woke
And drank my coffee, washed, put on my clothes;
On the way to work, I stopped and turned back,

But couldn't think what it was I had forgotten.
It was like the biplane from World War I.
Beyond the window, the tree was waving its arms.
A pilot from long ago, wearing my father's cap
And goggles, was waving his arms. Now I remember.
It was my father's dream, told to me as a child,
Put on like a coat that one day fits. I arise from
My window seat. Remember the child who wanted never
To grow up? The child has gone and found his way.

Steve Orlen, 1978

Saturday Night

The lock dreaming within the door
is being ambushed tonight. Someone
is trying to stab it in its sleep.
Its tiny metal ribs arch and shift
at the probe. Its moving parts tumble
over each other, then jam fast
in a self-embrace no burglar can force.
But this one is attached to the problem.
Absorbed in his work, he doesn't sense
the tenant's approach; not the shadow
which falls over his hand,
nor the form which follows it. Not until
a soft cough and a hissed *what's this?*
sends him racing down the service stairs.
Through the tiny metal cave
the key comes perfectly now—
the skyline of a city
with its delicate broken edges.

Anne Hussey, 1978

Ezra Pound's Eye

appeared to me just now
one eye his right eye
looking at me out of darkness

as I was about to fall asleep
aquamarine under the white eyelid
surrounded by heavy white eyebrows
lashes and wrinkles but it was
not a dull eye not
ancient but a hard glaring
hailstone under his white eyelid
why I ask do you look at me
with your right eye?
why do swallows hide in your sleeve?
and while we're at it
what does "scaled invention" mean?
and he glared back
pulling down on his forehead
a beret of black sequins
he opened a nut with one hand
and it was filled with shining worms
and I ran out
thin-footed
to touch the wind

Anne Hussey, 1978

Third Decade

After the Interrogation

There is the sack of skin, dark
or light, ready to give out
under small cunningly-applied pressures
its passage of blood
from the heart to the tongue.
There is firefall & gangrene,
there are forty-three days of interrogation
& a fifteen-year sentence in the works.
Plenty of time to dream in your cell
of a young woman's breasts:
the purple areolas deepening to black
at the nipples, of burying your head
between them & never coming up.
Death would be like that, you say—
something that makes you ache inside
the way a woman can make you ache.
Or a few sad fragments of speech
from *The Cherry Orchard* come back to you,
& you remember the first time you read it
how you wanted to cry, because it was true,
that sadness. Russia dying
into the twentieth century—what could have been
further from your life?—& yet Chekhov
was speaking only to you: telling you
he was once as scared as you were
of blank paper, of its stare, but just wrote
& wrote because all he wanted
was someone to talk to, that what was
writing anyway but someone talking
to someone he couldn't see.
How it came to you later, one morning
on Hoedjes Bay, up-coast from Capetown,
the wind driving the sand off the dunes
into your nostrils, your hair,
a few thick-necked cumuli
skudding inward toward land & no rain,
the waves crashing four abreast,
each one a mouth
talking & talking, slab after slab of language

heaved up from the sea—
& for the first time you knew
you were born to this life to write
in the open, to read the braille
surface of things & give emptiness
a face.
          Pigeons
scratching the cement in the cell-yard
wake you, but in your mind
you're back in Johannesburg,
that tree on State Street: the pigeons
underneath clucking like grandmothers
as they devour the pink clusters of fruit
they imagine have fallen only for them.
How they remind you of the guards—
all appetite & affability.
And yet, nothing like the guards
at all. Who are not birds, but only men
doing a job, & you
are the job.
                    And it's only now, finally
awake from this morning's beating,
that you see it: the window.
The guards have left the window open.
But not out of carelessness, & not for the air.
So.   All that blather about power
& how much of it the State can wield
over a person, when any child
could have told you—pain.
A ten-penny hose artfully employed,
a glass rod worked from the tip
of the penis to its root & then broken,
bending the arm past the elbow's
ability. . . . Enough pain
that they won't have to kill you, you'll
do it for them, *that* kind of power.
And that once dead, you are theirs.
Public. Molecular. Stripped of thought,
of its privacy, which terrifies them
as it once terrified you—the solitude
& particulars of moving through time.

Time, which goes only as far
as the window, which is four feet away
& is open & is seven flights down.
That everything you've written
since that morning by the ocean
is there, just past the window, saying
don't do it—though something
in your body is moving anyway, & no one,
not even you, has a right to stop it.
But your arms are too mangled to pull.
You'll have to help. You'll have to make it
on words alone this time, drag yourself
by the tongue to the window,
lean far enough out
& let go . . .
                    into a rush
of women's breasts, your wife, her breasts
sagging against her blouse as she bends
over the well in the courtyard at home
looking at her hair in the water. And in her hair
a pale-green comb of Malagasy tortoiseshell,
& you think, of all things, why that?
A comb. Something trivial & exquisite
your last thought on earth
as the cement shoves into you
so suddenly & so hard
it doesn't hurt—just the momentary
nausea, a few miserable syllables
coughed up with the blood, & then silence.
Silence by the well in Soweto. Silence
under the tree on State Street. Silence
with its boot in the door of your voice.

Lawrence Kearney, 1980

Globe

I spread my game on the cracked linoleum floor:
I had to play inside all day.
The woman who kept me said so.

She was middle-aged, drank tea in the middle of the day,
her face the color of dust layered on a table.

A high window let in alley light
to a two-room apartment.
Sofas and chairs bristled like hedgehogs
and made the back of my legs itch.
No red flowers on the windowsill. No radio.
Just waxy vines drooping over the tables,
a dome clock dividing time into fifteen-minute parcels.

What did I do all day?
Made card houses so frail
I had to turn my breath the other way.
Or colored the newspaper comic strips,
or wobbled across the floor in my mother's old pumps
with the aplomb of somebody drunk.

Enter my father at 5:15, dark and immediate,
finished with his shift at the factory.
He was hiding something behind his back.
He turned as I circled him,
keeping whatever it was out of sight.
Close your eyes and hold out your hand—
I touched a globe slotted on top for coins,
my hand shadowing the continents
like a cloud thousands of miles wide.
He put my finger over the state where we lived,
then handed me his loose change to fill the world with.

Memory's false as anything, spliced in the wrong parts,
queerly jumping. But better than forgetting.
We walked out into the soft light of October, leaves
sticking to our shoes like gold paper.
I was four years old and he was twenty-five,
same age as I am writing this.

Elizabeth Spires, 1981

Exhumation

For Elizabeth Siddall (1832–1862), wife of Dante Gabriel Rossetti

You shut me up in a cold box and buried me
just because I died   at first I thought
I'd never forgive you that
the turning away
the last of many desertions

I rotted   slowly and without anguish
gracefully
flesh falling from my arms   fingertips turning to mush
my teeth blossoming into a huge smile
     eight years I thought about my life among the living
     the afternoons slowly escaping through rose-stained windows
     the smoke of women's hair moving among men
     the dew rising from fields in solid, shining points

And in the end, my thoughts always returned to you, Dante
to the dissatisfactions
that had hovered between us like small grey clouds

Then   gradually   you fell away
into the cold blankness of time
became otherworldly so I could no longer understand
but your poems
your gift to me on the first day of my death
they stayed with me
they were there   next to my cheek
     something I could never say of you with your brothel nights
     and your distaste for my body—
     the possessing, I mean

Then   when I was only bone and no longer a treasure
you dug me up
rude jolting from the dream!
the terrible reawakening to trees and the color of the sky!
oh   the silence I screamed as light swarmed into my marrow
as you rifled me
taking the poems tied with my hair   bound in my skin
not looking into the sockets where my eyes had swum
     believing I was gone like a lightless traveller

> heartless   I wanted to call you
> inhuman as you stood above me all human and living
> a vulture   a circling black thing
>
> It was then that I clutched myself into a cold hard ball
> and prepared for the second gravesleep
> this time without any of the small attachments necessary
>   for a woman slighted in life
> this time with a hollow in my cheek

Elizabeth Spires, 1981

Courtesan with Fan

Auspicious night.
     The stars balance on poles
as a crescent moon, half-eaten,
rises out of the persimmon tree.

The dragon at the top of the sky
flails the universe

as if I were once more seven,
my mother binding my feet into delicate hooves.
I rocked like a boat, my feet two white moons,
two crescents of pain.

Half-woman, I languished in the sequestered bedchamber
till my body sprouted—
a swollen green shoot tender to strangers.

They handle me, paint
my shoulders with their tongues.

I breathe in the blackness of complete abandon,
as if I were diving for pearls,
     deeper, deeper,
my spiderfine silks changing to seaweed.

Always when it happens, I close my eyes.

My bones bend like watery willows.
The stars, tiny mourners, go out one by one.

Elizabeth Spires, 1981

78's

For Frank Bidart

Breakable; heavy; clumsy; the end of a side
the middle of a movement—or phrase
(the faults are obvious); surface noise;
one opera—three albums, four inches, thirty-three sides wide . . .

But under the noise, the surface, the elegant
labels, the bright shellac—Revolutions: Szigeti,
Schnabel, Busch, Beecham, Casals, Toscanini (*new '30s disc star at
sixty*);
all their overtones—understood, amplified, at hand:

Our Masters' Voices taking our breath,
revelations per minute, winding up in a living
room—turning the tables, taking off—moving: moving
faster (they make us think) than the speed of death.

Lloyd Schwartz, 1981

Self-Portrait

For Ralph Hamilton

"I was sitting in her living room,
looking very hard at the painting I had given her.
I asked her for a knife, and very deliberately
cut up the canvas. She was furious;
I told her, 'I'll paint you a good one.'

—Every painting is a self-portrait.

I always
straighten the pictures on people's walls . . .

I live at home,
painting while my parents are away at work.
I cook their dinner. It's a compromise,
but it's the only way I can afford to work;
better to compromise
my life.
            And if I suffer—
so much the better; not
easy.

They're amazingly patient—
my mother thinks I'm a 'great artist.'
My paintings are all over the walls,
mostly piled up against the window
in the dining room. (The dining room
hasn't seen the light of day in three years.)

I read a lot, when I'm not painting,
and play the piano—badly.
I'm fascinated by words. Some of my paintings
have words in them: AWAY . . .
GET WELL. In college,
I wrote my autobiography.

I've been commissioned to do a portrait—
I've done several;
                    but I shouldn't do them,
I don't know how. Every portrait
becomes just another painting . . .''

In your self-portrait,
the blinds are open, but you are looking
away; your eyes green, and enormous.
There is a sunny street outside—
grey and black shadows cover your face; your mouth
twisted with irony, or tenderness,
refusing to speak.
You say, "It's just another painting."

—A train disappearing over a hill;
a burnt-out house; two trucks colliding
in mid-air;
                your father; your mother; a baby;
a chair; a hand on a venetian blind . . .
"Every painting is a self-portrait."

Lloyd Schwartz, 1981

Yellow Light

One arm hooked around the frayed strap
of a tar-black patent-leather purse,
the other cradling something for dinner:
fresh bunches of spinach from a J-Town *yaoya*,
sides of split Spanish mackerel from Alviso's,
maybe a loaf of Langendorf; she steps
off the hissing bus at Olympic and Fig,
begins the three-block climb up the hill,
passing gangs of schoolboys playing war,
Japs against Japs, Chicanas chalking sidewalks
with the holy double-yoked crosses of hopscotch,
and the Korean grocer's wife out for a stroll
around this neighborhood of Hawaiian apartments
just starting to steam with cooking
and the anger of young couples coming home
from work, yelling at kids, flicking on
TV sets for the Wednesday Night Fights.

If it were May, hydrangeas and jacaranda
flowers in the streetside trees would be
blooming through the smog of late spring.
Wisteria in Masuda's front yard would be
shaking out the long tresses of its purple hair.
Maybe mosquitoes, moths, a few orange butterflies
settling on the lattice of monkey flowers
tangled in chain-link fences by the trash.

But this is October, and Los Angeles
seethes like a billboard under twilight.
From used-car lots and the movie houses uptown,

long silver sticks of light probe the sky.
From the Miracle Mile, whole freeways away,
a brilliant fluorescence breaks out
and makes war with the dim squares
of yellow kitchen light winking on
in all the side streets of the Barrio.

She climbs up the two flights of flagstone
stairs to 201-B, the spikes of her high heels
clicking like kitchen knives on a cutting board,
props the groceries against the door,
fishes through memo pads, a compact,
empty packs of chewing gum, and finds her keys.

The moon then, cruising from behind
a screen of eucalyptus across the street,
covers everything, everything in sight,
in a heavy light like yellow onions.

Garrett Hongo, 1982

Stay with Me

At six o'clock, most people
already sitting down to dinner
and the Evening News, Gloria's
still on the bus, crying
in a back seat, her face
bathed in soft blue light
from the fluorescent lamps.
She leans her head down
close to her knees, tugs
at the cowl of her raincoat
so it covers her eyes, tries
to mask her face and stifle
the sobbing so the young black
in the seat across the aisle
won't notice her above the
disco music pouring from
his radio and filling the bus.
He does anyway, and, curious,

bends towards her, placing a hand
on her shoulder, gently,
as if consoling a child
after the first disappointment,
asking, "Is it cool, baby?"

She nods, and, reassured,
he starts back to his seat,
but she stops him, sliding
her hand over his, wanting
to stroke it, tapping it instead,
rhythmically, as if his hand
were a baby's back and she
its mother, singing and rocking
it softly to sleep. The black
wishes he could jerk his hand
away, say something hip to save
himself from all that's not
his business, something like
"Get back, Mama! You a fool!"
but he can't because Gloria's
just tucked her chin over
both their hands, still resting
on her shoulder, clasped them
on the ridge of her jaw the way
a violinist would hold a violin.

He can feel the loose skin
around her neck, the hard bone
of her jaw, the pulse
in her throat thudding against
his knuckles, and still he wants
to pull away, but hesitates,
stammers, asks again,
"Hey . . . Is it okay?"

He feels something hot
hit his arm, and, too late
to be startled now, sighs
and gives in, turning his
hand over, lifting it, clasping
hers, letting her bring it

to her cheek, white and slick
with tears, stroking her face
with the back of his hand,
rubbing the hollow of her cheek
against his fist, and she,
speaking finally, "Stay with me
a little while. Till your stop?
Just stay with me," as her face
blooms and his shines
in the blue fluorescent light.

Garrett Hongo, 1982

Who Among You Knows the Essence of Garlic?

Can your foreigner's nose smell mullets
roasting in a glaze of brown bean paste
and sprinkled with novas of sea salt?

Can you hear my grandmother
chant the mushroom's sutra?

Can you hear the papayas crying
as they bleed in porcelain plates?

I'm telling you that the bamboo
slips the long pliant shoots
of its myriad soft tongues
into your mouth that is full of oranges.

I'm saying that the silver waterfalls
of bean threads will burst in hot oil
and stain your lips like zinc.

The marbled skin of the blue mackerel
works good for men. The purple oils
from its flesh perfume the tongues of women.

If you swallow them whole, the rice cakes
soaking in a broth of coconut milk and brown sugar
will never leave the bottom of your stomach.

Flukes of giant black mushrooms
leap from their murky tubs
and strangle the toes of young carrots.

Broiling chickens ooze grease,
yellow tears of fat collect
and spatter in the smoking pot.

Soft ripe pears, blushing
on the kitchen window sill,
kneel like plump women
taking a long, luxurious shampoo,
and invite you to bite their hips.

Why not grab basketfuls of steaming noodles,
lush and slick as the hair of a fine lady,
and squeeze?

The shrimps, big as Portuguese thumbs,
stew among cut guavas, red onions,
ginger root, and rosemary in lemon juice,
the palm oil bubbling to the top,
breaking through layers and layers
of shredded coconut and sliced cashews.

Who among you knows the essence
of garlic and black lotus root,
of red and green peppers sizzling
among squads of oysters in the skillet,
of crushed ginger, fresh green onions,
and pale-blue rice wine simmering
in the stomach of a big red fish?

Garrett Hongo, 1982

The Hongo Store
29 Miles Volcano
Hilo, Hawaii

From a photograph

My parents felt those rumblings
Coming deep from the earth's belly,
Thudding like the bell of the Buddhist Church.
Tremors in the ground swayed the bathinette
Where I lay squalling in soapy water.

My mother carried me around the house,
Back through the orchids, ferns, and plumeria
Of that greenhouse world behind the store,
And jumped between gas pumps into the car.

My father gave it the gun
And said "Be quiet," as he searched
The frequencies, flipping for the right station
(The radio squealing more loudly than I could cry).

And then even the echoes stopped—
The only sound the Edsel's grinding
And the bark and crackle of radio news
Saying stay home or go to church.

"Dees time she no blow!"
My father said, driving back
Over the red ash covering the road.
"I worried she went go for broke already!"

So in this print the size of a matchbook,
The dark skinny man, shirtless and grinning,
A toothpick in the corner of his smile,
Lifts a naked baby above his head—
Behind him the plate glass of the store only cracked.

Garrett Hongo, 1982

Forgetting Greek

Translucent prophylactic, shield, interpreter—
language, I peel you off, stout rubber glove
I no longer need. My hand
is no longer callused by field work.
I recognize its uses.

I never knew I'd pulled you on so far.
There I was one day elbow deep in a tongue,
fingers furrowed with the unexpected.
Out of my depth, I started to pull back.
The soapy water of an alien way,
scummed pool, Narcissus puddle to gaze into
enchanted, distracted a young attention from
the bleak centrality of self. But now
here is my own right hand, still mine, uncovered,
square-ended nail-bitten fingers tapping the keys
of the language they thought I'd forget.

Rachel Hadas, 1983

Kaleidoscope

You ask the source of these transparencies.
Although each speaker is another self,
all finally return and merge to one
composite whole from which each fragment's spun.
Names, gestures, seasons, every kind of weather
one's friends can lend while losing nothing—these
are all I've taken. What is there to fear?
Busily I stitch a gospel, match
the patchwork of a city day, or peer
through blue arcades a single twist of year
has turned past recognition. Help me out,
chorus of voices. You know who you are.
Change partners: still it comes down to the same
symmetry dancing on its head of pain.
Label those angels if you can. As, whose
eyes brimmed with loneliness; whose anger found
its edge in shifting razor glints of color:

yours? yours? I put the instrument down. Meet
an eye, a pair, another, then another.
What lifts itself to meet me's pure anxiety
that in a twinkle flickers recognition.
It nods: I see you through the far end of the eyescope,
the you-turn, eyesore, telelooker, thing
to measure with, to gesture with, to distance
and finally to dance to. Parts are bowing
in little v's of colored glass. They itch
to curtsey, twirl, and strut their stuff. They die
to form a pattern—even words. Begin.

Rachel Hadas, 1983

Once, Driving West of Billings, Montana

I ran into the afterlife.
No fluffy white clouds. Not even stars. Only sky
dark as the inside of a movie theater
at three in the afternoon and getting bigger all the time,
expanding at terrific speed
over the car which was disappearing,
flattening out empty
as the fields on either side.

                              It was impossible to think
under that rain louder than engines.
I turned off the radio to listen, let my head
fill up until every bone
was vibrating—sky.

                    Twice, trees of lightning
broke out of the asphalt. I could smell
the highway burning. Long after, saw blue smoke twirling
behind the eyeballs, lariats
doing fancy rope tricks, jerking silver
dollars out of the air, along with billiard cues, ninepins.

I was starting to feel I could drive forever
when suddenly one of those trees was right in front of me.
Of course, I hit it—

branches shooting stars down the windshield,
poor car shaking like a dazed cow.
I thought this time for sure I was dead
so whatever was on the other side had to be eternity.

Saw sky enormous as nowhere. Kept on driving.

Susan Mitchell, 1983

The Dead

At night the dead come down to the river to drink.
They unburden themselves of their fears,
their worries for us. They take out the old photographs.
They pat the lines in our hands and tell our futures,
which are cracked and yellow.
Some dead find their way to our houses.
They go up to the attics.
They read the letters they sent us, insatiable
for signs of their love.
They tell each other stories.
They make so much noise
they wake us
as they did when we were children and they stayed up
drinking all night in the kitchen.

Susan Mitchell, 1983

Tent Caterpillars

For Nathaniel, 1900–1968

All afternoon you worked at cutting them down.
Branch after branch tossed
into the heap. You had your ceremony. Old pants. The pipe.
The pipe rested in the cleft of the tree.
When the pile got big enough, you threw the kerosene.

Now the woods are clouded again. You forgot
the world could be this messy.

Air thickens into leaves, the leaves into worms.
Behind the barn, overnight, it seems,
tents have spread out in the apple trees.

There's work for you. So you come back
in your pants old as dirt. With a pipe heavy as stone.
No time to lose. Whatever is rotten,
whatever won't hold the weight of another season,
you hack down. There's one moment, though,

when you feel almost sorry for them.
The tents break into flame and the small, black
pieces of anguish crawl
out into the grass. Those that get away, well,
you let them get away this time.

Susan Mitchell, 1983

Dreams of Johnson Grass

If for a night my tongue would sleep.—*Dara Wier*

each night I float into levels of cislunar
space like some weightless astronaut
harvesting dreams that will betray me
if only for a night my mind would sleep
but each night a new world
and landscapes of mysteries
where I orbit inside stories
of family members I've longed to forget

strange shapes blossom and fade
like thickets of brake and nettle
fields of chickweed, stringy mustard
horsetail and crabgrass, once planted
they are fertile but often troublesome
the stingy profiles of next of kin
the generations of distant relatives
creeping home

cousins thrive on the moonscape
of my sleep space

standing in long secular lines
like winter wheat or scrawny maize
their voices raspy as crickets
others are plump as milkweed
and seed my dreams with coarse and pithy
children who call me by my maiden name

Jo-Jo, hey Jo, repeated again and again
in a bed of light, handsome Uncle Phillip
beckons me into his arms
I rush past my mother's clicking tongue
past cross-eyed Cousin Rosa
her frowning face dark as a prune
now my dreamscape is riddled with ghosts
I am Great-aunt Dora jumping trains
outside of Fulton Mo with her bandit lover
or Fanny slumping over the supper table
the shock of poison surprising her heart

I am pulled toward Warren, my eighth-grade love
first cousin removed and no longer
too serious to step across bloodlines
his skin is perfect as obsidian
we finally meet at dawn and I awaken
in the imagined space of his arms
my tongue cannot fill the vacancy with words
they bloom so quickly
these rangy faces from my fragmented past

if only poems could come so easily
so perfectly, like a lock
of white hair above an innocent face
or the meaningless spirals of deep sleep
where I am pure Pulitzer and ride the wind
swirling like pollen
from Solomon's-seal or swaying
above a splendid field of witches-breath

Colleen McElroy, 1984

With Bill Pickett at the 101 Ranch

he was wilder than a wolf when he
brought down a steer with his teeth

but working the 101 was a damned sight better
than riding herd through Kansas winters

snow higher than the haunches of his best horse, Spradley
and his face, if not burnt summer black, matching his saddle

"damn that colored feller can bull-dawg," they said
when the bull whip-snapped his body like a twig

the crowd of Shoshone stragglers and coon-tailed
mountain men cheered this bronze cowpoke

who earned his keep by his teeth, but when he turned
show biz and rode the 101 with Tom Mix and his Ralston

Straightshooters, camp bosses with red beards and grey eyes
grew nervous to see just what he could do

what he could do was judge the angle of light
against ground swell of mud from gate to center post

despite old rope burns that hummed memories to his bones
he listened as calves moaned in the holding pens

and longhorns bellowed at the sound of his footsteps as if
they knew how his hands were rubbed raw against horns

how he bit the bill's lip until the beast caved in
and how his own blood smelled worse than puke and dung

worse than the scent of death in the air
or the crowd cheering bull against man
and hoping, dear God, the beast would win

Colleen McElroy, 1990

For Want of a Male a Shoe Was Lost

in 1944 the fitting room was a fluoroscope where bones
of school-bound children danced inside their caskets
of new shoes like halloween cutouts of skeletons caught

in the silent green frost of x-ray machines—all belly and
mouth ready to suck in feet buttoned-up for the onslaught
of death-dealing playgrounds and arithmetic seating

that brown box was the lasting room where the shape
of shoes was determined by metal forms and how uppers fit
linings and eyelets and groove

always with room to grow—the outsoles like running
boards on a Ford and heels clunky as a horse's hooves
tooled to stand the strain on all parts worn

every fall I walked in someone else's shoes
my discomfort of fit explained by news of a war
or feet that, the shoe merchant said, would last forever

(meaning next winter) with stitches to keep me out
of little slips of tongue—that arch-guard of memory
which, if let loose, readily told the world where I stood

but never with the right fit of merchant's shoe
or style to match my mental picture of elegant slipper
which never matched the fluoroscope's ghostly dancing bones

under that machine even cheap shoes could seem handmade
the man turned the dial until my feet were bleached green
and when mama approved of how they had grown bone dainty

she peeled off dollar bills: one for my father in Normandy
one for an uncle in the Pacific or a cousin's government check
the money folded as tight as those new shoes which dressed

me in eyelets that could not see and tongues tucked
away from naked light while the bony shadows of my black feet
danced all alone—radiating green in the moonlight machine

Colleen McElroy, 1987

Elegy for Thelonious

Damn the snow.
Its senseless beauty
pours a hard light
through the hemlock.
Thelonious is dead. Winter
drifts in the hourglass;
notes pour from the brain cup.
Damn the alley cat
wailing a muted dirge
off Lenox Ave.
Thelonious is dead.
Tonight's a lazy rhapsody of shadows
swaying to blue vertigo
& metaphysical funk.
Black trees in the wind.
Crepuscule with Nelly
plays inside the bowed head.
"Dig the Man Ray of piano!"
O Satisfaction,
hot fingers blur
on those white rib keys.
Coming on the Hudson.
Monk's Dream.
The ghost of bebop
from 52nd Street,
footprints in the snow.
Damn February.
Let's go to Minton's
& play "modern malice"
till daybreak. Lord,
there's Thelonious
wearing that old funky hat
pulled down over his eyes.

Yusef Komunyakaa, 1984

Landscape for the Disappeared

Lo & behold. Yes, peat bogs
in Louisiana. The dead
stumble home like swamp fog,
our lost uncles & granddaddies
come back to us almost healed.
Knob-fingered & splayfooted,
all the has-been men
& women rise through nighttime
into our slow useless days.

Live oak & cypress
counting these shapes in a dance
human forms aren't made for. Faces
waterlogged into their own
pure expression, unanswerable
questions on their lips.

Dumbstruck premonitions rise
from the heckle-grass
to search us out.
Guilty, sings the screech owl.
I hear the hair keeps growing
in the grave. Here
moss lets down a damp light.

We call back the ones
we've never known, with stories
more ours than theirs.
The wind's low cry
their language, a lunar rainbow
lost among Venus's-flytraps
yellowing in frog spittle & downward mire,
boatloads of contraband
guns & slot machines dumped
through the years.

Here's this lovely face so black
with marsh salt. Her smile,
a place where minnows swim.
All the full presence

shiny as a skull under the skin.
Say it again—we are
spared nothing.

Yusef Komunyakaa, 1986

Starlight Scope Myopia

Gray-blue shadows lift
shadows onto an oxcart.

Making night work for us,
the starlight scope brings
men into killing range.

The river under Vi Bridge
takes the heart away

like the Water God
riding his dragon.
Smoke-colored

Viet Cong
move under our eyelids,

lords over loneliness
winding like coral vine through
sandalwood & lotus,

inside our lowered heads
years after this scene

ends. The brain closes
down. What looks like
one step into the trees,

they're lifting crates of ammo
& sacks of rice, swaying

under their shared weight.
Caught in the infrared,
what are they saying?

Are they talking about women
or calling the Americans

beaucoup dien cai dau?
One of them is laughing.
You want to place a finger

to his lips & say "shhh."
You try reading ghost talk

on their lips. They say
"up-up we go," lifting as one.
This one, old, bowlegged,

you feel you could reach out
& take him into your arms. You

peer down the sights of your M-16,
seeing the full moon
loaded on an oxcart.

Yusef Komunyakaa, 1988

Camouflaging the Chimera

We tied branches to our helmets.
We painted our faces & rifles
with mud from a riverbank,

blades of grass hung from the pockets
of our tiger suits. We wove
ourselves into the terrain,
content to be a hummingbird's target.

We hugged bamboo & leaned

against a breeze off the river,
slow-dragging with ghosts

from Saigon to Bangkok,
with women left in doorways
reaching in from America.
We aimed at dark-hearted songbirds.

In our way station of shadows
rock apes tried to blow our cover,
throwing stones at the sunset. Chameleons

crawled our spines, changing from day
to night: green to gold,
gold to black. But we waited
till the moon touched metal,

till something almost broke
inside us. VC struggled
with the hillside, like black silk

wrestling iron through grass.
We weren't there. The river ran
through our bones. Small animals took refuge
against our bodies; we held our breath,

ready to spring the L-shaped
ambush, as a world revolved
under each man's eyelid.

Yusef Komunyakaa, 1988

Venus's-flytraps

I am five,
    Wading out into deep
        Sunny grass,
Unmindful of snakes
    & yellowjackets, out
        To the yellow flowers
Quivering in sluggish heat.

Don't mess with me
       'Cause I have my Lone Ranger
Six-shooter. I can hurt
   You with questions
      Like silver bullets.
The tall flowers in my dreams are
   Big as the First State Bank,
      & they eat all the people
Except the ones I love.
   They have women's names,
      With mouths like where
Babies come from. I am five.
   I'll dance for you
      If you close your eyes. No
Peeping through your fingers.
   I don't supposed to be
      This close to the tracks.
One afternoon I saw
   What a train did to a cow.
      Sometimes I stand so close
I can see the eyes
   Of men hiding in boxcars.
      Sometimes they wave
& holler for me to get back. I laugh
   When trains make the dogs
      Howl. Their ears hurt.
I also know bees
   Can't live without flowers.
      I wonder why Daddy
Calls Mama honey.
   All the bees in the world
      Live in little white houses
Except the ones in these flowers.
   All sticky & sweet inside.
      I wonder what death tastes like.
Sometimes I toss the butterflies
   Back into the air.
      I wish I knew why
The music in my head
   Makes me scared.
      But I know things
I don't supposed to know.

I could start walking
　　　& never stop.
These yellow flowers
　　　Go on forever.
　　　　　Almost to Detroit.
Almost to the sea.
　　　My mama says I'm a mistake.
　　　　　That I made her a bad girl.
My playhouse is underneath
　　　Our house, & I hear people
　　　　　Telling each other secrets.

Yusef Komunyakaa, 1992

My Father's Love Letters

On Fridays he'd open a can of Jax
After coming home from the mill,
& ask me to write a letter to my mother
Who sent postcards of desert flowers
Taller than men. He would beg,
Promising to never beat her
Again. Somehow I was happy
She had gone, & sometimes wanted
To slip in a reminder, how Mary Lou
Williams' "Polka Dots & Moonbeams"
Never made the swelling go down.
His carpenter's apron always bulged
With old nails, a claw hammer
Looped at his side & extension cords
Coiled around his feet.
Words rolled from under the pressure
Of my ballpoint: Love,
Baby, Honey, Please.
We sat in the quiet brutality
Of voltage meters & pipe threaders,
Lost between sentences . . .
The gleam of a five-pound wedge
On the concrete floor
Pulled a sunset

Through the doorway of his toolshed.
I wondered if she laughed
& held them over a gas burner.
My father could only sign
His name, but he'd look at blueprints
& say how many bricks
Formed each wall. This man,
Who stole roses & hyacinth
For his yard, would stand there
With eyes closed & fists balled,
Laboring over a simple word, almost
Redeemed by what he tried to say.

Yusef Komunyakaa, 1992

Ballad of the Swimming Angel

In the dusty light of an attic room he woke,
pulled on jeans and a leather jacket and went out.
He saw huge tanks rise and fall in steel cages,
saw the skyline shimmer, begin to smoke.
And saw the poor, bunched at corners, wait-
ing for the light, dreaming of higher wages.

Hello to the cop blowing into cupped hands;
a wave to each clerk inside each store,
moving quietly as fish. He turns to the ocean.
He arrives. But something about the sand's
flat color sends him flying along the shore
as the surf makes its endless corrections,

and wind stirs the bright flakes of sleep
on the water's surface. It is so still
so early, and the poor angel forbidden to swim.
But, naked, he dives between green pleats
of wave, kicks down deeper and deeper, until
he wakes in the dusty light of an attic room.

Jeffrey Skinner, 1985

Rolling in Clover

For Laura

My daughter practicing her vowels at dawn
woke us happy. All week the sky pressed—
humidity 95. Today the sun is pure, held
by the light air gently, breatheable.

Poplars throw small change in the wind.
Milkweed spore fly past my blanket,
delicate aliens looking for the new world.
A kingfisher pauses, pinned to a cloud

like a furious thought, seconds before
the kill. . . . This horizon's a cup of leaves
I try to fill with vision, though the trees
are enough, and the clouds revolving

as on a sphere of glass. *Description's
a way in, that place where things come back
to themselves,* I write, then hold the page
up for the wind to erase. Oh, any weather

can heal, but if the scene's too pretty
to write, and you are suddenly as happy
as you'll ever be, get down in the clover,
father, down in the green sunlight, and roll.

Jeffrey Skinner, 1985

Thoreau's Fossil Lilies

We find ourselves in a world already planted. . . . —A Writer's Journal

Years later, critics would be saying
You had to look just off, in parallax,
To see your own face in that
"Filthy pond."

They'd be calling you names
They could not afford to gauge

Their own needs by.
Truth was, you'd found

These lilies; they made you forget
John Brown, sweet gale,
And pickerel dart.
They were rock, but they were

Flowers, laughing at the corners
Of their centuries;
Frozen at one time
But now, little cauldrons

Of history.
I imagine you bending over them,
Suddenly amazed.
Putting them into your satchel

To hoard wonder and shyness
As if they were wives.
And on the banks of the pond,
An old choir

Of elms, singing from
The frozen earth as you passed.
To the rest of the world, friend,
Those lilies were fresh.

Brenda Hillman, 1985

Cleave and Cleave

The lifeguards have gone in for the season;
their stilted chair
still looks out like an egret on the strip of sand
that's cluttered with artifacts: one thong,
sun-lotion bottles, the sunken
pockets of footsteps filled with trash.
I stop on the cliff and stare down at the lake
that builds its private character in the off-season,
imagine sunbathers skiing now,

taking their introverted goldenness
down the bright slopes.

In the parking lot,
a young couple embraces, coming from
the shoulders of the lawn with picnic remnants,
and finding their Buick he presses her against it
and she tilts her sun hat toward him so it
catches the light like a last
phase of the moon—she knew
it would do that—

The cold takes up this image
and shatters it; she stumbles, touches
his arm, buttons her top button
and for a second the absent bathers seem to come back
surrounded by plastic shovels and towels,
and with bland curiosity, trying
to understand that this happiness
is not unlike their own.

Minutes later, another couple
comes out screaming from the shadows,
and running along a white line, he spins
her around: "Why don't you
say something to me, say something to me!"
They have driven a long way to fight in public;
the absent lifeguard is hurrying over,
the girl puts her fists over her eyes,
runs around the car like a flag
on the antenna,
just circles without form, but I keep
walking, so I don't know what will happen later.

Spinoza, who ground lenses, looked
past the bestial shapes of furniture,
past the powdered glass
to human nature
and believed every substance is infinite, but
love may be extreme, and the mind
distracted by this can ruin
the perfection of God;

and there are those
linguistic twins *cleave* and *cleave,*
which stem from opposites, meaning
split and stick, two same
sounds arriving like coincidence
in the day or in a breath:
I felt such freedom when you walked away;
I won't stop loving you, even in death.

Brenda Hillman, 1989

Quartz Tractate

Let's see now. The idea of reverse seeing:
whereby a plant will be seen for instance
by the ground. My friend saw backward into this world.
In the tent, where wisdom is eaten
by the snake, the poem sees into us.
Days and nights of this;
the job of the living is to be seen through.

As a swallow, harrowing the raptor, dives
in and out of the forbidden ovals,
seeming to derange them,
only to realize the raptor doesn't care,
goes on with its crenellated flight,
so I entered the mystery
and the mystery ignored me—

Baffled by death, I sought her in myself,
sometimes—often—speaking to her.
Now that has faded a little—

But still.
Why doubt that she goes on helping?
We were both everything in this. It wasn't
that she was the crystal and I was the ashes.

I go to the hill where "she" lies and see
it's true. Things borrow splendor.
In the shine off the back of a very large beetle

on the driest hill where so much is in bloom.
Even the serpentine pebbles in the cracks bloom,
even the cracks bloom.
The beetle crawls across one and goes on
lifting its legs as high as it can—

Brenda Hillman, 1992

Mighty Forms

    The earth had wanted us all to itself.
The mountains wanted us back for themselves.
The numbered valleys of serpentine wanted us;
that's why it happened as it did, the split
as if one slow gear turned beneath us . . .
Then the Tuesday shoppers paused in the street
and the tube that held the trout-colored train
and the cords of action from triangular buildings
and the terraced gardens that held camelias
shook and shook, each flower a single thought.

Mothers and children took cover under tables.
I called out to her who was my life.
From under the table—I hid under the table
that held the begonia with the fiery stem,
the stem that had been trying to root, that paused
in its effort—I called to the child who was my life.
And understood, in the endless instant
before she answered, how Pharaoh's army, seeing
the ground break open, seeing the first fringed
horses fall into the gap, made their vows,
that each heart changes, faced with a single awe
and in that moment a promise is written out.

However we remember California later
the earth we loved will know the truth:
that it wanted us back for itself
with our mighty forms and our specific longings,
wanted them to be air and fire but they wouldn't;
the kestrel circled over a pine, which lasted,
the towhee who loved freedom, gathering seed

during the shaking lasted, the painting released
by the wall, the mark and hook we placed
on the wall, and the nail, and the memory
of driving the nail in, these also lasted—

Brenda Hillman, 1993

C. T.'s variation

some springs the mississippi rose up so high
it drowned the sound of singing and escape
that sound of jazz from back
boarded shanties by railroad tracks
visionary women letting pigeons loose
on unsettled skies
was drowned by the quiet ballad of natural disaster
some springs song was sweeter even so
sudden cracks split the sky / for only a second
lighting us in a kind of laughter
as we rolled around quilted histories
extended our arms and cries to the rain
that kept us soft together

some springs the mississippi rose up so high
it drowned the sound of singing and escape
church sisters prayed and rinsed
the brown dinge tinting linens
thanked the trees for breeze
and the greenness sticking to the windows
the sound of jazz from back
boarded shanties by railroad tracks
visionary women letting pigeons loose
on unsettled skies
some springs song was sweeter even so

Thulani Davis, 1985

telepathy

when in the house
something became clear
they listened to the wind
which could not be told
from the ocean

she felt the house move
like people stepping
he heard a night noise
just a sound in a new house

they loved each other anyway
late they hid together
under sheets blankets talk

they loved each other
as best they could
at any moment
something became clear

they shut up and sighed
because something true
disappointed them
made them sad
they never knew the same things

what infant wailing
on one side of the earth
he heard as himself
she thought a glass pane
creaking
always at this time

Thulani Davis, 1985

A Fly on the Water

I
It is eating me.
It is everything hungry in the world,
And wants me, and I'll tell you, I don't mind.
The women I meet are soft fire;
At night,
Space rattles in my heart;
Your voice,
That muffled angry breathing.

My fathers shuffle the sky; odor of pine trees,
Dark sandy soil. I am lonely,
And think of those sad mystical men in their dark hats,
Who made God's noise when they prayed,
Made it louder in their goose-down beds,
When they clapped their wives' ears
And heard God's drum measuring their bones.

II
A child opens his arms
In the summer heat. With eyes half closed,
He feels the life spilling inside him.
Small and pale on the grass,
He looks almost cruel, he is so happy.

The tree shakes, and God falls out;
Lifetimes of skin and longing stroll naked in the street.
Because it is all I know, I do this;
My text, a joke of the flesh, like eyesight, hummingbirds,
Anything that soars.

III
Stillness spreads from your face
Like ice knitting on a pond.
When it breaks, will God stream past my ankle
Darkly, or as a pool of deadly light?

A fly skates on nothing, on tension:
On something as abstract as a prayer, or as love.

Paul Zweig, 1985

The End Circulates in the Wide Space of Summer

I
We hardly speak.
You have been here so long
You are like another leg or arm.
We trot across the ice,
Approach the book, and enter it.
You read the text,
I try to hear what you are saying.

The sky shivers,
A bird moves across it like a flexible blade.

So it began.

II
The end circulated in the wide space of summer,
With sawing of small insects, bubbles
Clustering in ponds.

I try to hear what you are telling me,
But the smile of an invisible cat consumes the sky;
That singsong call of young girls
Jumping rope is death's nursery rhyme.

III
Where in this endless room
Is the one who loves me,
The hissing of her silks?

We talk of God, his mica angels,
His book of living wormed in rock.
We have what lasts,
And the soft perishable mind, which doesn't.
We have the spacious word
Where nothing begins, and goes on beginning,
As long as we live.

Paul Zweig, 1985

Poem

I don't know if I can bear this suddenly
Speeded-up time. I pull the blinds
And it is morning: white flowers gleam
Under the linden leaves; the cathedral's red dome
Dwarfs the timid skyline across the river.
A town like any other: cars grinding
Over the cobbles, the perishable mosaic of fruits
And vegetables in front of small stores.
The dead look on indifferently from their green horses,
From their pedestals, where they receive the homage of pigeons.
There are no old men, only brown, mocking boys
And girls dancing out of their clothes.
The old men loiter, silent and transfigured,
In museums, nursing their small immortalities.
Can you smell it? The car fumes, coffee, breath,
Old leather, urine, a young woman's perfume.
It smells of youth, death, sleepless nights;
It never looks up, doesn't see
The blank enduring looks of the statues;
And yet it is a kind of poem.
But now I'm thinking of those green men
Concentrated in their single, undistracted movement,
Their heads pulled belligerently back
While they tug on the reins of a bronze horse,
Their eyes like termites boring holes in nothing,
Because they have hit on the one gesture
That will never fail of completion,
Their whole perishable selves squeezed into
A green eroded look that chuckles at the stupidities
Of springtime and young girls, from their own springtime
Of ominous, wretched, sour verdure.
Oh, the egotists, the zany gods commemorating
One or another of the lies men tell
To garnish their forgettable lives: the legends,
Bibles, enormous whisper rising like a cloud of bees,
A shimmer of golden motes,
And their honey! Fluid as water, transparent, sweet,
So that anyone who tastes it forgets father and mother,
Lover, children, money, cancer, failed hopes.
Oh, the cunning among stones, turning the fear of life into the

love of life.
The statues, all to their monomaniacal greenness,
Enjoy the joke, although they don't laugh,
Or even smile; while the girls gather their black hair into a bun,
And the boys call out mysterious passwords of blood and sperm
And a sweet smell comes from the fruit stands, where cherries,
Apricots, peaches, plums soften and sag;
A cloying liquid wets the tilted boxes, darkening the sidewalk.
Soon it will be evening.

Paul Zweig, 1989

Krakow and the Girl of Twelve

The dog downstairs is howling back
to the old country. My grandmother
bends to pick up the hoe
drags it, sun-slant, down toward the field
kicking the blunt end
up, until it flashes.
     Wolves, her mother said,
slipping through the gate.

Marianne Boruch, 1985

My Son and I Go See Horses

Always shade in the cool dry barns
and flies in little hanging patches like glistening fruitcake.
One sad huge horse
follows us with her eye. She shakes
her great head, picks up one leg and puts it down
as if she suddenly dismissed the journey.

My son is in heaven, and these
the gods he wants to father
so they will save him. He demands I
lift him up. He strokes the old filly's long face
and sings something that goes like butter

rounding the hard skillet, like some doctor
who loves his patients more
than science. He believes the horse

will love him, not eventually,
right now. He peers into the enormous eye
and says solemnly, I know you. And the horse
will not startle nor look away,
this horse the color of thick velvet drapes
years and years of them behind the opera,
backdrop to ruin and treachery, all
innocence and its slow
doomed unwinding of rapture.

Marianne Boruch, 1989

Buick

On the rusting fender of the old
Buick, I lay down my head
and watch the field blur with flowers,
clouds in their noble boredom
drag the sky bluer as they

pass. But this is winter, and I'm inventing
what leads me out of my life,
a set of intricate pulleys, gift
of the boy genius in the basement—my brother
maybe—who begged off school to get on with things.

Nothing shakes this field: eventually
shadows sift into grass, earth
cools by evening, and not like music.
This Buick was my father's. I'm sure of that.
He drove it here drunk. He parked it here

gracelessly, and sat with years
bunched behind him, which is to say
he thought of nothing, squinting down

the glare. So my family figures things. We stop
until the fury dwindles down to ash, what

would be bone. Perhaps an archaeologist could
find us; one xeroxes an unreadable something
through winter's half-afternoon. I see
that narrow room, his face moon-desolate
and slack. As for the fitful shaft of light

pure as fishhook, it is grief
or something worse.

Marianne Boruch, 1989

from *Black Holes, Black Stockings*

Round Sunday. Wooded plains underwater, seaweed, urchin, sea-horse,
and the gelatinous os implanted on the rock. Its rose madder flowered—
the myth of the toothed—a sunrise of tresses to cilialike ease in its prey.
The rose flash sweeps the waterwind. And when the mouth puckers, cor-
dovan, doorless, it confounds. Smoke-moon enamel from a distance, tra-
versed by speedboat the sea jells into membrane, petrol green on descent.
We thought silverfish until the boat stopped and we saw seaweed re-
flected as silver-leafed poplars. Cricket island. White flowers of summer
like winter, milksnake feeding on the paproot. Nimble light we crack
diving. The horn of the troubadour is forced outside the self in shape,
where we bob a brief note in the after-dive. Allowing someone else to
panic where I was playing, taking the whole hillside for a friend from far
asea, the sea grapes, emptying its vacuum of charged bubbles from a
double-prowed cruiser, both wakes. Day necklace, night glass unwob-
bling. The first inch is forgiveness. The noun that is cleaned disappears.
Putting up with their manifestations like smoke in our faces already
turned from that elegant perfume, like flamingos who wandered north
from the tropics, we concentrate on abiding. Our body casts out a cypress
root as logos while the unharnessed gray whale escapes the muffle of the
ocean wash: fattest cows and youngest heifers, beautiful electronic im-
ages, the loneliness of their small good hearts. All the nights go on by
hand, journey of a thousand knots, milk again learning nothing. Ha!
Priests! Red lamp poles, muscadet sky: upside down. Parakeets in the
afterlife, silverpious, pass to slope the world. Pre-Alps, perched villages,

memories, as when you fall asleep god exists. Some visible keeping still, opium, oyster, the unswirling of the smoke unswirling the mollusk, signals us to daily with the frail. The sound of a nut opening, brain-wake.

Olga Broumas and Jane Miller, 1985

There's a song of privacy that begins Go away Go away, and stills the mice and the porcupine too, crouched at the door as you fiddle the keyhole. Lizards, asleep, roll a little farther from your bed, spiders hand over hand in the moonlight climb as if to it, holding the rim of the amber pot until a signal to scale down again. Alone, alone, the sweet golden beads with their interior lights guided by destiny guiding night travelers beyond, back or askew into the not-here, the knot in the crossroads where they must tire and halt like a girl caught in her hair where the teeth of the combs are too tight together, throwing the comb down and sleeping deeply on the tangle, worsening it, happy in dream. Tomorrow it will be snipped away, tomorrow the porcupine will startle you from the fig tree, pointing its tears at you or, worse, beyond to some backfire or allergen thriving among the geraniums; snag, broken egg, broken string. But now the silent choral, the poppy growing sunflower-size in a vibration Chagallesque, tipped in flare burning in, tranquil candelabra with its funny rhyme glowing inside you.

Olga Broumas and Jane Miller, 1985

A Parable

The stone strikes the body, because
that is what stones will do.
The wound opens after the stone's kiss,
too late to swallow the stone.
The wound and the stone become lovers.
The wound owes its life to the stone
and sings the stone's praises.
The stone is moved. At the stone's center,
a red hollow aches to touch the wound.
The gray walls of its body tear open
and the wound enters to dwell there.

A stranger picks up the stone
with the wound inside and carries it
with him until he dies.

Gregory Orr, 1973

Gathering the Bones Together

For Peter Orr (1951–1959)

When all the rooms of the house
fill with smoke, it's not enough
to say an angel is sleeping on the chimney.

1. *A Night in the Barn*
The deer carcass hangs from a rafter.
Wrapped in blankets, a boy keeps watch
from a pile of loose hay. Then he sleeps

and dreams about a death that is coming:
Inside him, there are small bones
scattered in a field
among burdocks and dead grass.
He will spend his life walking there,
gathering the bones together.

Pigeons rustle in the eaves.
At his feet, the German shepherd
snaps its jaws in its sleep.

2.
A father and his four sons
run down a slope toward
a deer they just killed.
The father and two sons carry
rifles. They laugh, jostle,
and chatter together.
A gun goes off,
and the youngest brother
falls to the ground.
A boy with a rifle
stands beside him, screaming.

3.
I crouch in the corner of my room,
staring into the glass well
of my hands; far down
I see him drowning in air.

Outside, leaves shaped like mouths
make a black pool
under a tree. Snails glide
there, little death-swans.

4. *Smoke*
Something has covered the chimney
and the whole house fills with smoke.
I go outside and look up at the roof,
but I can't see anything.
I go back inside. Everyone weeps,
walking from room to room.
Their eyes ache. This smoke
turns people into shadows.
Even after it is gone,
and the tears are gone,
we will smell it in pillows
when we lie down to sleep.

5.
He lives in a house of black glass.
Sometimes I visit him and we talk.
My father says he is dead,
but what does that mean?

Last night I found a child
sleeping on a nest of bones.
He had a red, leaf-shaped
scar on his cheek. I lifted him up
and carried him with me, though
I didn't know where I was going.

6. *The Journey*
Each night, I knelt on a marble slab
and scrubbed at the blood.
I scrubbed for years and still it was there.

But tonight the bones in my feet
begin to burn. I stand up
and start walking, and the slab
appears under my feet with each step,
a white road only as long as your body.

7. *The Distance*
The winter I was eight, a horse
slipped on the ice, breaking its leg.
Father took a rifle, a can of gasoline.
I stood by the road at dusk and watched
the carcass burning in the far pasture.

I was twelve when I killed him;
I felt my own bones wrench from my body.
Now I am twenty-seven and walk
beside this river, looking for them.
They have become a bridge
that arches toward the other shore.

Gregory Orr, 1975

The Weeds

On the lawn, beside the red house
she taught me to slice deep
circles around dandelions
with the sharp point of my trowel
so when I pulled them
the taproots come up too.

She wore a blue dungaree jacket,
her braided hair
tied up in a paisley bandanna.
We crouched there near each other,
mother and son, digging in silence
in the dusk of late summer.

Gregory Orr, 1980

Elegy

For James Wright

Not only doesn't the Ohio
stop tonight, it moves more
easily under the stars,
under the barge lights.
And in my veins
blood, though heavy
with sorrow, still flows.
And below the Catskills
the Hudson keeps flowing—
my own river, that's deeper
than anyone dreams
with its rich secret
of fish intact under
all that sewage and grief.

On the Hudson's far shore
there's a chestnut—
my own tree—a plank
fort hid in its branches.
Your poems taught me it
was there, though it's nothing
like your own tree by your own
river's bank—that sycamore,
pure thing so like the simple
word you sought, tree
from which the gray bark
peels and drops until
it stands half
in rags, half in radiance.

Gregory Orr, 1986

The Mother

I was fourteen and it was my birthday party in Haiti. When they brought the cake in, I stood and went to my room. I lay on my bed and wept—the sorrow was real, but so was the calculation my mother would follow, that she would enter and sit on the bed and ask why I was crying.

And I would say my brother's name, he whom, two years before, I had killed, although by accident. And somehow I would have tricked her into forgiving me. But when I spoke his name, she sat awhile in silence, stroking my forehead, and then she rose and left.

So for me nothing was changed. It was as if somehow my brother and I existed inside one of those thick glass globes that enclose a wintry pastoral—two children, bundled against cold, building a snowman while around them white flakes swirl.

How odd for the crying boy to cling to an image of cold in the tropics. At first you think the coldness stands for his mother who cannot comfort him, but you must realize she is also the mother of the dead boy—her son taken violently from her; and how that made her feel no one will ever know, because, in a few months, she herself will suddenly die. At the age of thirty-six to lie down in a bower of ashes.

And I, her son, am older than her now, older than she is in any image of her I carry inside me. So, it must by *my* task to understand and comfort *her*, to tell *her* story, because only I know what's there at the heart of her grief; I see it, no matter what nacreous layers time may wrap it in: a piece of dust, a snowflake, no living thing.

Gregory Orr, 1988

Eulogy for a Hermit Crab

You were consistently brave
On these surf-drenched rocks, in and out of their salty
Slough holes around which the entire expanse
Of the glinting grey sea and the single spotlight
Of the sun went spinning and spinning and spinning
In a tangle of blinding spume and spray
And pistol-shot collisions your whole life long.
You stayed. Even with the wet icy wind of the moon

Circling your silver case night after night after night
You were here.

And by the gritty orange curve of your claws,
By the soft, wormlike grip
Of your hinter body, by the unrelieved wonder
Of your black-pea eyes, by the mystified swing
And swing and swing of your touching antennae,
You maintained your name meticulously, you kept
Your name intact exactly, day after day after day.
No one could say you were less than perfect
In the hermitage of your crabness.

Now, beside the racing, incomprehensible racket
Of the sea stretching its great girth forever
Back and forth between this direction and another,
Please let the words of this proper praise I speak
Become the identical and proper sound
Of my mourning.

Pattiann Rogers, 1986

The Objects of Immortality

If I could bestow immortality,
I'd do it liberally—on the aim of the hummingbird,
The sea nettle and the dispersing skeletons of cottonweed
In the wind, on the night heron hatchling and the night heron
Still bound in the blue-green darkness of its egg,
On the thrice-banded crab spider and on every low shrub
And tall teasel stem of its most perfect places.

I would ask that the turquoise skimmer, hovering
Over backwater moss, stay forever, without faltering,
Without disappearing, head half-eaten on the mud, one wing
Under pine rubbish, one floating downstream, nudged
And spit away by foraging darters.

And for that determination to survive,
Evident as the vibration of the manta ray beneath sand,
As the tight concentration of each trout-lily petal
On its stem, as the barbed body curled in the brain

Of the burrowing echidna, for that intensity
Which is not simply the part of the bittern's gold eye
Most easily identified and remembered but the entire
Bittern itself, for that bird-shaped realization
Of effective pressure against oblivion, I would make
My own eternal assertion: Let that pressure endure.

And maybe this immortality can come to pass
Because continuous life, even granted to every firefly
And firebeetle and fireworm on earth, to the glowing clouds
Of every deep-sea squirt, to all electric eels, phosphorescent
Fishes and scaly bright-bulbed extensions of the black
Ocean bottoms, to all luminous fungi and all torch-carrying
Creatures, to the lost light and reflective rock
Of every star in the summer sky, everlasting life,
Even granted to all of these multiplied a million times,
Could scarcely perturb or bother anyone truly understanding
The needs of infinity.

Pattiann Rogers, 1989

The House Destroyed by Fire

Arrangement preserves. The way a calm tureen
of fish soup hubs our circle or a stripped oak
table anchors its room. Order, unseen
at first, settles like fine ash. Our talk
glimmers. A candle set behind glass
fences the crickety dark.
                         Not knowing what
went first, I have to imagine chaos:
a tongue licking out from the wood stove that
hissed *kitchen* all day, a spark in the new
socket chasing its wire like a fuse,
rags waking to a slow smolder below
the floorboards. More details sprout—quick shadows
jagging papered walls, the rows of spice tins
exploding, reams of typing like wild
cabbages of flame.
                         Once it's begun,
description stuffs itself sick. That charred field,

blanched by now, is probably filled with bugs.
The fieldstone lattice that cut out each odd square
of room has faded under weeds. Only dregs
remain: littered, still tantalizing, as the fear
of loss grows ragged, peculiar, seedy.
Spare work set our table, arranged the taste
that opens that time now. Let memory
give way to bare articulate space.

Don Bogen, 1986

The Last Installment

Remember our lamp, its frowzy Victorian hat
of a shade? Nights in that drafty stained-glass parlor
I'd read aloud in the fringed glow while you sewed.
We might have been someone's great-grandparents, or characters

in those fat books. Imagine our ancestors caught in them through
the long dark sea of the nineteenth century,
coming back month after month like letters home
from the Empire's most distant outpost. The day

is bright. Master is sitting chatting in the sitting room
and has called for early tea. I fancy the daughter
of the vicar has caught his quick eye. Outside, the broad heath
glowers as always. I spied someone poaching over there,

your lordship, grouse hunting he were, out beneath
last night's full moon. Good work, Barker, do keep
us alerted. In the shop at the curve of High Street
they are ringing a small bell for me. I want it to stop,

I don't want to bring in the great bolt of silk that
is taller than I shall ever be. Let the dance fail,
the heroine weep in last year's gown. Let the ship
sink, all its letters lost at sea, at the crazy wheel

the cabin boy at last. And our ancestors stumbling up
from steerage, blinking, in the cold salt light

of a dim empire of words, gathered by the crossing-sweep
for the factory girl so lovely and illiterate.

Don Bogen, 1986

In My Own Back Yard

1
July, I'm dozing in sun on the deck,
one thrush is singing among the high trees,
and Li Po walks by, chanting a poem!
He is drunk, he smells unwashed,
I can see tiny lice in his hair,
and right through him
a brown leaf in the yard
flips over flips
again lies still
all this time
no wind.

2
From behind November glass I watch the wind
truck all its winter furnishings
item by item into my yard.
In a dusty raincoat my neighbor
throws a tennis ball, over and over,
to exercise his police dog.

Sometimes I feel like one of the world's bad headaches,
sometimes I think I get no closer
to what I have wanted to mean
than the gumshoe calling
"Testing"
up to the bugged ceiling . . .

You can try to put words to a mood
or tell yourself to ignore it,
but what kind of message is coming
from the chickadee, dapper
in his black mask and skullcap,
grooming himself on the big pine's branch-tip?

His music is small and monotonous,
but it's his own.

3
I am turning pages in lamplight.
Outside, above blue snow, in February dusk,
in the double world of glass,
more pages flip, like wings—
this merging of me and the world
done with mirrors and windows.

4
Hunting for duck eggs at the end of March
I watch three mallards and a speckled female make
a tight flotilla on the swollen creek.

The dog barks at her counterpart
on the other bank. Nothing is green
the way these mallards' heads are green.

Empty-handed, I turn back to the house.
Small waterlights
play on the underbranches of the ash. High up
the sycamore lifts its light-peeled limbs
against a turning sky.

5
Late May. Summer coming on again. I think
Li Po may not be back. Worried about
the world's end, as, I realize
I have been most of my life,
I take my work outside
and sit on the deck, distracted.
It was a day like this, I think,
in Hiroshima.
Distracted.
There must be something in the pinecones
that the chickadees—there's another one.
What's this that's snowing down? Husks, pollen,
freckle-sized petals from our wild cherry trees!

We sneeze and plant tomatoes. Ultimatums. The world
comes close and goes away

in rhythms that our years
help us begin to understand.

We haven't long to live.
And the world? Surely the world . . .
A deep breath. Sunshine.
Mosquitoes, bird calls, petal-hail.

David Young, 1986

As It Is

There was a basket of fruit between us.
We lasted with the shade
at opposite ends of the picnic table.

What was passing on did not appear
to age the foliage of afternoon.
The wind combed the moist leaves.

We kept feeling our long breaths would take
root; not a wrinkle of pain on our faces.
There was nothing we wanted to say.

Light filtered through the upper clouds.
Houses on the far hill reflected
an arrangement of insects and birds.

There was a basket of fruit between us.
We lasted with the shade
at opposite ends of the picnic table.

Occasional children blushed, clinging
to the vines. Everywhere, ferns
and mosses absorbed the knocking of limbs.

We kept feeling our long breaths would take
root; not a wrinkle of pain on our faces.
There was nothing we wanted to say.

Ralph Angel, 1986

Tatters

Sure, the need was simple
and the effort crowds the Silver Dragon piano bar.
We know how much of us is missing. We know the camaraderie
of surrender, upright in our chairs. "Well, friend,
the next life is not about to appear tonight
though it offers its usual promises in the tunes of that
piano, ice tumbling through sleeves of rose-colored glass,
our ideal voices, the pout she must have learned

in California. We might say it's every bit of 1:17 a.m."
These things happen. Toss an arm around the thick of it,
but what to do about this unabashed momentum?
At first it's easy: man with factory squint
kicks ass of man wearing a black shirt, and then is inclined
to punch his face in. Pick and choose, "Dust the sucker,"
the good, the merely ugly, that random
kitchen shatter, the whole gala hubba hubba

parading into the background. On the wall
hangs the old Chinese *lung*, another wingless power of the air.
Like the girl who scratches a thumbnail across
her slick, lamé blouse, the pulse of unspoken noises
still jockeys for favors. Sure, one decent grope deserves
the same in return, but the truth is too often frivolous.
"Anyways," he blusters, "Billy's gonna buys us a drink."
"Tell me. Tell yourself to me."

Ralph Angel, 1986

Take Care

When a man dies, he does not die just of the disease he has; he dies of his whole life.—
Charles Péguy

Our neighbor Laura Foley used to love
to tell us, every spring when we returned
from work in richer provinces, the season's
roster of disease, bereavement, loss. And all
her stars were ill, and all her ailments worth
detailing. We were young, and getting up

into the world; we feigned a gracious
interest when she spoke, but did
a slew of wicked imitations, out
of earshot. Finally her bitterness drove off
even such listeners as we, and one by one the winters nailed
more cold into her house, until the decade crippled her,
and she was dead. Her presence had been
tiresome, cheerless, negative, and there was little
range or generosity in anything she said. But now that I

have lost my certainty, and spent my spirit in a waste
of one romance, I think enumerations have their place,
descriptive of what keeps on keeping on. For dying's nothing
simple, single; and the records of the odd demises
(stone inside an organ, obstacles to brook,
a pump that stops, some cells that won't, the fevers making
mockeries of lust) are signatures of lively
interest: they presuppose
a life to lose. And if the love of life's
an art, and art is difficult, then we
were less than laymen at it (easy come
is all the layman knows). I mean that maybe
Laura Foley loved life more, who kept
so keen an eye on how it goes . . .

Heather McHugh, 1987

I Knew I'd Sing

A few sashay, a few finagle.
Some make whoopee, some
make good. But most make
diddly-squat. I tell you this

is what I love about
America—the words it puts
in my mouth, the mouth where once
my mother rubbed

a word away with soap. The word
was *cunt*. She stuck that bar
of family-size in there
until there was no hole to speak of, so

she hoped. But still
I'm full of it—the cunt,
the prick, short u, short i,
the words that stood

for her and him. I loved
the things they must have done,
the love they must have made, to make
an example of me. After my lunch of Ivory I said

vagina for a day or two, but knew
from that day forth which word struck home
the more like sex itself.
I knew when I was big I'd sing

a song in praise of cunt—I'd want
to keep my word, the one with teeth in it.
Forevermore, and after I was raised, I swore
nothing but nothing would be beneath me.

Heather McHugh, 1987

20-200 on 747

There is rain on the glass but it all disappears
when I look toward the curve on the world.
(The here and now is clear, I mean, so we
can't see it.) In an airplane, chance

encounters always ask, So what
are your poems about? They're about
their business, and their father's business and their
monkey's uncle, they're about

how nothing is about, they're not
about about. This answer drives them
back to the snack tray every time.
Phil Fenstermacher, for example, turns up

perfectly clear in my memory, perfectly attentive to
his Vache Qui Rit, that saddest cheese. And now an interlude while we
commiserate: it takes what might
be years to open life's array

of incidental parcels—mysteries
of red strips, tips, and strings, the tricks
of tampons, lips of band-aids, perforated notches on
detergent boxes, spatial reasoning milk-carton quiz and subtle

teleologies of toilet paper.
Mister Fenstermacher is relieved
to fill his mind with the immediate
and masterable challenge of the cheese

after his brief and chastening foray
into the social arts. We part
before we part; indeed
we part before we meet. I sense

the French philosophers nearby,
I hope not in the cockpit (undermining
meaning, as they do, or testing aerial translation's
three degrees). They think

we're sunk, we're sunk, in our little
container, our story
of starting and stopping. Just
whose story is this anyway? Out of my mind

whose words emerge? Is there a self the self
surpasses? (Look at your glasses, someone
whispers. Maybe the world
is speckled by

your carelessness and not its nature.
Look at your glasses, if you want

to see.) Who says? We're not
alone, the town down there

grows huge, one tiny runway will
engulf us. Is the whisperer
Phil Fenstermacher, getting a last word in
before the craft alights? I look

at my glasses. I see
what he means. They're a sight.

Heather McHugh, 1988

What Hell Is

March 1985

Your father sits inside
his spacious kitchen, corpulent
and powerless. Nobody knows
how your disease is spread; it came
from love, or some
such place. Your father's bought
with forty years of fast talk, door-to-door,
this fancy house you've come home now to die in.
Let me tell you what
hell is, he says: I got this
double fridge all full of food
and I can't let my son go in.

•

Your parents' friends
stop visiting. You are a damper on
their spirits. Every day you feel
more cold (no human being
here can bear
the thought—it's growing
huge, as you grow thin).
Ain't it a bitch, you say, this
getting old? (I'm not sure
I should laugh. No human being
helps, except

suddenly, simply
Jesus: him you hold.)

•

We're not allowed
to touch you if you weep or bleed.
Applying salve to sores that cannot heal
your brother wears a rubber glove.
With equal meaning, cold or kiss
could kill you. Now what do I mean
by love?

•

The man who used
to love his looks
is sunk in bone
and looking out.

Framed by immunities
of telephone and lamp
his mouth is shut,
his eyes are dark.

While we discuss despair
he is it, somewhere
in the house. Increasingly
he's spoken of

not with. In kitchen
conferences we come
to terms that we
can bear. But where is he?

In hell, which is
the living room.
In hell, which has
an easy chair.

Heather McHugh, 1988

Spilled

The waiter dropped a tray of glassware and
the din of conversation stopped as if
in shock at competition. Not until
that moment were we quite aware

of what a roar the ordinary made,
not until a knife of other noise could cut
right through it to the greater emptiness,
right through to zero, there

where no one for a moment said
a blessed word. And then the other
nothings started coming back, the hum of small talk
rising gradually to flow and to recirculate, its rhythms

swelling up and out of the hole in the story to make
the story normal once again, the cruise control back on,
the life as a career in which we can afford,
as usual, to fail to hear.

•

The restaurant's a show of selves
collected into dreamy twos and fours;
their fantasies are fed, their livings made;
the hundred couples can pretend

they are accustomed to a cook and maid
and then, by some consensual agreement (because none
can really *be* the monarch of the model) they ignore
the commonplace, with its proximities, the many

foreign monarchies that munch and belch
next door. Each buys a little
privacy, say three by five, and dreams that he
is different. The dream is purchased at the price

of never seeing being from above or from
a distance, somewhere difference might disappear,
and all of what is being said
might add up to one animal's

far-flung identifying cry: for all we know
that's how a God is reached, in whose
broad synaesthesias of sympathy a blood
need not be bright or red if spilled as speech . . .

Heather McHugh, 1988

Hay Scuttle

The holes in the floor of the barn loft
were cut for dropping shucks to the stalls.
Pile an armload on the opening
and stuff them through. The cow
is already eating as the rest
splash on her head. The fodder sweet
as tobacco is pushed down for the horse.
Light from below rises with manure
and warm cud-breath.
And bleach from the horse's bed.
Dark up here with the dead grass
and cornsheller, except for the trapdoors.
Only way out to the sun is down,
through the exquisite filth.

Robert Morgan, 1987

Ghosts in the Carpet

Aunt Pearlie draped her rug across
the fence as though raising a tent
or effigy of her parlor,
and taking up the old shovel
handle slammed the heavy vestment
until it smoked, until it
puffed cloud after cloud out across
the weeds, settling on flowerbeds,
garden rows, the dusts of winter
and the leaner spring, the sheddings
and fibers, the fine silts of human

habitation caught between
the weft threads, motes and tiny crusts,
microscopic morsels, little
prisms fogging over the wet
summer vegetation as she
swung and swung again, freeing lint
and fine detritus to fade like
phantoms in the hard sun, flogging
away the soil and hair and rust
from the fabric's memory. And
after the rug was bright, the colors
new, she beat still more the patterns
with her ancient stick until they
sparkled and exhaled no more dirt,
but hung pure and breathless, heavy
in the breeze, their ghosts given up.

Robert Morgan, 1991

A Dream of Glass Bangles

Those autumns my parents slept
warm in a quilt studded
with pieces of mirrors

On my mother's arms were bangles
like waves of frozen rivers
and at night

after the prayers
as she went down to her room
I heard the faint sound of ice

breaking on the staircase
breaking years later
into winter

our house surrounded by men
pulling icicles for torches
off the roofs

rubbing them on the walls
till the cement's darkening red
set the tips of water on fire

the air a quicksand of snow
as my father stepped out
and my mother

inside the burning house
a widow smashing the rivers
on her arms

Agha Shahid Ali, 1987

In the Mountains

Somewhere
without me
my life begins

He who lives it
counts on a cold rosary
God's ninety-nine Names in Arabic

The unknown hundredth he finds in glaciers
then descends into wet saffron fields
where I wait to hold him

but wrapped in ice
he by-passes me
in his phantom cart

He lets go of the hundredth Name
which rises in calligraphy from his palm
Fog washes the sudden skeletons of maples

Farther into the year by a broken fireplace
I clutch the shiver of a last flame
and forget every Name of God

And there in the mountains
the Koran frozen to his fingertips
he waits

farther much farther into the year
he waits for news of my death

Agha Shahid Ali, 1987

Trying to Begin

Here you are once more, sitting at a table,
hands folded and ankles crossed, the most
ordinary of mornings and absolutely nothing to do.
And slowly, neither awake nor asleep,
you start to feel
you must have been lost a long time in the cells of paper,
a faint tinkle of dust
coming back to life in the world of the ear.
The coffee is cold,
yet always the same white ground and the same ghostly figures
weaving toward a distant light,
and lines groping for some opening in the crushed wall,
and lines that glisten like the snail's whereabouts
down to this wet sheaf
that might have just arrived, so heavy and fresh,
from the wheat farmers in regions of ice and cloud.
Or maybe just a layer of sodden leaves
left on the doorstep by the nightlong rain.

Robert Mezey, 1987

The Stream Flowing

I remember the creek that ran beside the golf course,
slow and black over rocks; patches of snow;
withies of willow streaming out in the wind,
born to it and, I imagine, bowing and scraping.

I would sometimes sit there shivering and looking out
at the flagless frostbitten greens, the naked trees
that bordered the bleak fairways and a sky
the ashen color of longing and disappointment.

Early winter, it was. And then I remember
the girl I brought there one night—the summer after?
We lay deep on the grassy bank, almost hidden,
and I touched her warm secret hair for the first time.

I can still hear the sound of water pushing by us,
the sound of her breath in my ear as I touched her there,
my stiff boyish hand trembling against her belly.
Her name was June. I could feel a pulse where I touched.

There were little lights in the breathing darkness around us.
Her eyes were closed and I was looking past her
at nameless summer stars and pulsing fireflies
and what must have been houses far off in the night somewhere.

Nothing else happened there. We were afraid,
and lay in the matted crush of the maidenhair
and chilly rivergrass. We could smell the night
and see the willow cascading over our heads.

I remember the last time I went there, alone and older,
three or four winters later. The clear water
was still flowing, now between snowcovered banks
and white fields stretched away to the hem of the sky.

One day melts into another and into years,
twenty years that flowed on and lost themselves in the sea.
Where is June, and the boy that she held to her body
on that bank once? Well, useless to think of her now,

and useless to think of the boy, by now a man—
each with a husband or wife, in a house far off
in the midst of another life, where I remember
the fern verging that stream and the stream flowing.

Robert Mezey, 1987

Thirty-six Poets

After Sakai Hōitsu

Some are drunk. Some are mumbling.
Many are solitary, each in his way fixed.
They are all happy over their very good number,
an easy square; its root six,
itself a lovely number, exponential chrysalis.
And if, in the array of patterns
taken from nature—clouds, spider webs, starfish—
we might yet find a true square
not one of these thirty-six, not the one
whose square is on his sleeve or heart, cares.

My old group, my buddies, the Math Team
would measure our drunks by booming
the quadratic formula, gleaming
with rum, slopped over some parents' living-room
rug, like these bards in their curtained cabal.
No one of us flubbed our password,
the drinking song, that poem of radicals
pressed in our brains, no gauge at all, absurd.
Minus b plus or minus the square root of
b squared minus four a c over two a.
Now even sober I lose those cancelled lines of youth
and drunk I am easily distracted, say,
by the discriminant, the bee-squared et al.
Concentrating on minutiae, I am lost in the well-
folded sleeve of the great poet's silk kimono,
lost on the silkworm's trail winding through Japan
and wonder, drunk, watching my steps split by Xeno,
drunk, wonder what led me to the simple numerical plan
and then away like dust in the path of a paper fan.

Judith Baumel, 1988

Mandolin

Because the Byrds were on his car
Radio singing *My Back Pages*,
My friend remembered the guitar
He smashed before he dove off stage

Into the crowd of high school faces
He hated. "Jerks and small-town jocks
In letter jackets, their straight-laced
Cheerleader promqueen dates. We wrecked

Two amps that night to get good loving,
Respect. What else did we want then?
I turned and watched our drummer shove
His set right off the risers, spun

And tossed my Fender at the speakers.
So much for all the crap I took
From coaches, teachers, north-side greasers,
Anyone who didn't like my looks."

He shifted into third, too hard.
"So who cares now. I graduated,
Couldn't afford a new guitar.
Soon all the songs I knew were dated."

"Yeah," I said, "I made gigs too,
Played trumpet on those call-and-answer
Riffs in a blue-eyed soul review,
Sweet licks to draw the couples closer

Across the free-throw line, our spot
Dim for the last dance, slow fade . . . .
But I wanted to move them, not
Just help some local hood get laid.

You know what I was like? Long-haired,
Too hip to smile, jeans always torn,
Nervous around adults, a spare
Joint in the case under my horn."

"Shut up," he said. "You're thirty-four,
I'm older. Why should we still care
Who put us down, or what we wore
Or were?" He let me out. Upstairs

I turned the radio on to static,
Off, picked up the mandolin
I found in my grandmother's attic
Cupboard, forgotten, with her pin

(A nickel silver lyre and stave)
And portrait of the Norwich Girls'
Mandolin Orchestra. Too grave
For such a kid, her fingers curled

On the neck, she stared, not at the glint
Of studio light on the lens,
But toward the frame, at the thumbprint's
Brownish whorl, as if she sensed

How she would hold the picture, bend
Years later toward a self so fast
Receding it seemed all ornament,
Soft grace note, nothing more. Past

Mending, I thought, when I undid
The cloth case, found the neck unstrung,
The pegs frozen. But she'd just died,
My first death, and it seemed wrong

Not to try some elegy,
So I tinkered, got it fixed, then lied
And said I practiced. Finicky
To tune, sweet toned, no amplified

Harsh declaration of the self,
It asked such delicacy. Four years
Ago I took it off the shelf,
Restrung it again, oiled the gears,

Because I'd dreamt I was that boy
Who didn't dance, stood near the speakers,

Forgot the concert band for Sly
Stone's trumpet charts, new sneakers

For black boots and a leather jacket.
In the dark gym, I saw my face
As grave, intent as hers, but lacking
In my unease all her grace.

An older man watched from the bleachers.
He kept his tweed coat buttoned, frowned,
And checked his watch. A coach, a teacher—
I couldn't place him—a chaperone?

Out in the emptying parking lot,
He stared into the rearview mirror,
Uncertain, as if he forgot
What it was that brought him there.

Hands in pockets, I was too nervous
To ask his name, and turned my back
As if indifferent or embarrassed.
I woke to the echo of a sax

And trumpet when the last chord dies,
Trembling as on a mandolin's
Twin strings, sustained, not quite on key . . .
Like my friend's anger or my own

Memory that loiters, shy,
Among the lunch lines, lockers, amps,
Unsure what I wanted or why
I still don't think I've got it. I damped

The strings, retuned, and tried to sound
The triplets of a jig. Not yet.
Again. My fingers faltered, found,
Then broke time on the narrow frets.

Jordan Smith, 1988

Twilight with Xs

A boy walking home in twilight.
Early spring, school almost out.
A low sun throws orange patches
on the row houses he knows by name.
He is late although not by much
and happy although not so
he knows it, throwing a bottle cap
up and a little ahead so he can easily
walk under it. He catches every one,
even the last above the porch light
before going inside where no one
will be mad at him and he climbs
the steps. By now you have wanted to go back,
to say something about yourself, about twilight
and happiness but he quickens
and will almost forget you,
the man coming toward him on the street.
Seen from his desk, the houses
he has just walked beside seem far away,
shrunken with small overlapping
shingles and you want to say you have
forgotten this and every house but not
the orange patches, not the bottle cap,
not the desk where he makes an X
on a piece of paper. Then another
and another until the paper is almost
full and some unite with others
forming bigger Xs and the paper
seems covered with one big X.
You were happy, you were and it is twilight.

Dean Young, 1988

Rothko's Yellow

What I don't understand is the beauty.
The last attempts of the rain, my shoulders
aching from all afternoon with the ladders
and the hour with her. I watch the rainbow

until I have to focus so hard I seem
to create it. Thinking of her watching
this storm, wanting him. This lightning.
This glut in the gutters. Now only
the yellow left. Now the blue
seeped out. The purple gone. The red
gone. People downstairs playing Bach,
the quiet, attenuated Bach. She must
have tried and tried. The holes drilled in.
The small man in the movie who looked
like laughter would kill him. The carnation
farmer who left snared birds for the woman
he loved. Who would hang himself after
stitching her ribbon to his chest.
What I don't understand is the beauty.
I remember the theatre in Berkeley where
we sat eating cucumbers, watching the colossal
faces played over with colossal loss.
I would get off early and meet her outside,
her hair always wet. All last night
I listened to the students walk by until 3,
only the drunk left, the rebuffed and
suddenly coupled. What did I almost
write down on the pad by my bed
that somehow lowered me into sleep? One morning
when she and I still lived together,
the pad said only, cotton. Cotton.
Sometimes it's horrible, the things said
outright. But nothing explains the beauty,
not weeping and shivering on that stone bench,
not kneeling by the basement drain.
Not remembering otherwise, that scarf she wore,
the early snow, her opening the door
in the bathing light. She must have tried
and tried. What I don't understand is the beauty.

Dean Young, 1988

In a Net of Blue and Gold

When the moored boat lifts, for its moment,
out of the water like a small cloud—
this is when I understand.
It floats there, defying the stillness to break,
its white hull doubled on the surface smooth as glass.
A minor miracle, utterly purposeless.
Even the bird on the bow-line takes it in stride,
barely shifting his weight before resuming
whatever musing it is birds do;
and the fish continue their placid, midday
truce with the world, suspended a few feet below.
I catch their gleam, the jeweled, reflecting scales,
small dragons guarding common enough treasure.
And wonder how, bound to each other as we are
in a net of blue and gold,
we fail so often, in such ordinary ways.

Jane Hirshfield, 1988

Justice without Passion

My neighbor's son, learning piano,
moves his fingers through the passages
a single note at a time, each lasting an equal interval,
each of them loud, distinct,
deliberate as a camel's walk through sand.
For him now, all is dispassion, a simple putting in place;
and so, giving equal weight to each mark in his folded-back book,
bending his head towards the difficult task,
he is like a soldier or a saint: blank-faced, and given wholly
to an obedience he does not need to understand.
He is even-handed, I think to myself,
and so, just. But in what we think of as music
there is no justice, nor in the evasive beauty of this boy,
glimpsed through his window across the lawn,
nor in what he will become, years from now, whatever he will become.
For now though, it is the same to him:
right note or wrong, he plays only for playing's sake
through the late afternoon, through stumbling and error,

through children's songs, Brahms, long-rehearsed, steady progressions
as he learns the ancient laws—that human action is judgment,
each note struggling with the rest.
That justice lacking passion fails, betrays.

Jane Hirshfield, 1988

For the Women of Poland: December 1981

I think of you standing
at the crossing of two streets,
where even the leaves have turned
accomplices of the cold.
You yield of yourselves
a patience, a hunger,
as other women might, at market,
offer a simpler crop:
robust ears of corn,
potatoes with green-sprouting eyes.
Everywhere there are lines,
people hoping for butter, or freedom,
or meat.
There are cards
with names printed on them
to be sold—cigarettes for flour,
playwrights for engineers.
It is a kind of love, your fingers
grown raw rubbing the wool of your coats,
the bark of these trees;
to touch anything
by now like touching yourself.
And the days draw on inevitably
as those lights of a once-great city
that tell you now stop, now go,
long after you've made up your minds
to stay stubbornly on,
grinding out an old music
on a hand-cranked gramophone
of a heart.

Jane Hirshfield, 1988

Compulsion as the Critical Element
in a Defined Perversion

To become acquainted with such a self as this
watching warily through the window half-
silvered by the encroaching dark—the night
only, no symbol, no vast reverberation fearsome
in far-reaching relevance—such a self as this
man trampling the late tulips and early
ferns fiddling their little heads above the loam,
was never matter of moment for her. She welcomed
only men of mere mystery, left the lust alone.

The weather alters often enough. The world
of wind and wetness suffices itself and soon
repeats. Wait for a warm day, and evening
will come. Wait for frost. It creeps
along the stems of little grasses and holds
its stiffening phallic folly long enough.
Then goes with the weather wherever.

She never thinks about it. Birds whisper
their prattle, meaningful enough.
No wonder she closes the windows, the blinds.

Bin Ramke, 1989

Buchenwald

Like the last laugh calved by innocence—*Aimé Césaire*

An orange butterfly trying to drink the tears
of an alligator drove the beast blinking
back to the swamp; the event means nothing
beyond itself and is random as words which mean
only their own use, for instance,
the German for *beech grove*, also subject
and title for a lovely little landscape
by Klimt, *um 1902*: useless innocence gathers
in the form of words like the children

of prostitutes accumulating the last
praxis of passion, accumulating

like clouds on the horizon. *Mon dessein
en est pris*, wrote Racine somewhere
(*Phaedra*), which is to say the design
is taken, which is perhaps, the translator
would say, to say my decision is final.
Design is not decision, nor is tragedy
random, nor is translation less than noble
in intent, whatever its traduction.
To reassemble into resemblance is something
and drives rough beasts in the manner of children
with sticks and stones into the swamp,

into the innocence of the original. The design,
the tailor says, of it is taken. You may go,
your dark suit will fit you tomorrow
and much mourning becomes us. But
we mostly mourn not people but possibilities
while the crepy skies descend most humbly
upon the day, upon the evening meal of wounded women
and mangled men who tried to talk to each other.
Their dense surrender dark as fruit
on the table, pits and seed and assorted
tangibles causing teeth to crack, teeth of the careless.

Let us bite into something solid for once
and consider the dark words—*négritude* being now
abandoned, the politics of simple sound lost,
of second world wars and third-world policies
and the exotic Francophone politics of Martinique,
for instance; the word traduced. And my own surrounding,
sometimes French-speaking, people spoke
in something passing for innocence

of *colored people* except when the needs
of anger produced *nigger* (from the French
nègre), in defense of darkness. Meanwhile
in a wood where the Brothers Grimm collected,
the smoke of a new form of fashion rose
from another oven. Save us,

Gretel cried, from the obliterating hunger,
huge and cute, of innocence. Or else just let
me and my brother go back into the forest dark
and deep, the lovely long white stems, the *Buchenwald.*

Bin Ramke, 1989

Married Love

As they sat and talked beneath the boundary trees
In the abandoned park, neither one mentioning
Her husband, or his wife, it seemed as though
Their summer shadows had detached themselves
In the confusion of those thousand leaves: but no more
Than they could call those shadows back from the air,
Could they ignore the lives they had undone,
And would undo once more that afternoon
Before giving in to what they knew, had always known.
And yet, in turning away, what they would say was not
That thing, but something else, that mild excuse
That lovers use of how things might have been
Had they met somewhere else, or in some better time,
Were they less like themselves than what they are.

Sherod Santos, 1989

Death

After Elizabeth Bowen

Although great in passing, although suddenly enlarged
    The frightened heart puts up its proud defense,
        Still, it always leaves you feeling
     A little smaller somehow, and living becomes a little
        Meaner then, necessitous, and preoccupied
With harder pleasures, like the lives of the poor.

It's as though your childhood house had been gutted
    By fire, the blackened walls left standing,
        The windows gaping under an open sky,

And suddenly one day you find yourself standing out
　　On the lawn without the heart or ambition
To rebuild. And in that hour, with its one idea

Of releasing you from some part of yourself, you think
　　You can see it unfolding there: how the maple trees
　　　　That line the yard are all cut down,
　　The land itself sold out in parts, how before
　　　　Too long small apartments will appear
In a long red row, each one a home for someone

You don't know. And after dark, where once was silence,
　　The maples' shadows drawn slowly across
　　　　The grass by a moon in counterpoise
　　Against the night, you find, instead, a string
　　　　Of porchlights have come on like stars,
And the bluish glow of television screens has filled

The windows from street to street. And then it happens
　　That in your mind a gate will click, a door swing
　　　　Shut, and bicycling children drift home
　　Like birds from the avenues and the birdless dark,
　　　　Until your childhood house seems gone
For good into the dead center of some memory's glow.

But years from now, when the smell of spring is still
　　Sweet in the air, or when snowdrops are beginning
　　　　To gather under the palings, when the blue
　　Autumn first blurs the narrow streets, or the low
　　　　Sun in winter dazzles the windows gold,
You'll discover inside, in that vague way you're still

Drawn to the air, that something has remained, something
　　Which, now silent and unseen, still touches
　　　　The heart. And there is someone, too,
　　Someone perhaps just returning from work, who will
　　　　Pause a moment, in sorrow or love, a hand
On the apartment gate, but not to wonder: What was here?

Sherod Santos, 1989

Near the Desert Test Sites
(Palm Desert, California)

For Logan and Renée Jenkins

Unlike almost everything
Else just surviving here
In summer, poison flowers
Flourish in this sweltering
Heat, tangling like blown
Litter in fences around
The trailer parks and motel
Pools, and turning the islands
Pinkish-white between
Divided lanes of freeway,
Where all day long against
The burnished hubbub of U-
Haul trucks and automobiles,
Off-the-road vehicles and
Campers, the oleander shakes
Its brightly polished pocket-
Knives, as at the motorcade
Of some ambassador hurrying
Through a village of the poor.
And every day by late after-
Noon the overwatered lawns
Around the shopping mall
Still burn off brown, their
Pampered opulence upbraided
By the palms' insomniac
Vision of one ineffable apoc-
Alyptic noon. But the smell
Is somehow sweeter than
That makes you think, a dry
Lemon-sweetness, as if some-
Where nearby wild verbena
Has been forced to leaf
By a match held up to each
Bud—and the silo-skyscraper
Holiday Inn at the famous
Resort "Where the Horizon
Ends" could almost be that

Match the way the heat
Sloughs off it like after-
Burn. And yet, because
Of the way the sun in-
Tensifies everything, one
Always has the feeling there
Is much less here than meets
The eye: the halcyon blink
Of a shard of glass, a Lear-
Jet wafted into vapor out
On the tarmac's run, the way
Common quartzstone gives
Off heat which seems to come
From inside itself, and not,
In fact, from that more-
Than-imaginably-nuclear sun
Which every morning starts
Up so illusionless, and every
Evening slow-dissolves
On the blue and otherwise
Planetary hills, like a Valium
Breaking up on the tongue.

Sherod Santos, 1989

Fourth Decade

The Continental Divide

I couldn't explain it to my husband,
who was squaring his papers as we drove
through the Carolina orchards.
So many ladders, left out in the rain
long after the picking season,
caught his attention, but the other
was a task to imagine. I pointed to the sign
that read Eastern Continental Divide
and lifted my foot off the accelerator
as we crossed over. The fields stretched easily
in both directions and there was no difference,
no natural landmark. He looked at the road ahead
as if he expected its surface to alter.
I told him we were talking about water—
this is where rivers change course,
where one source can divide, become two
and move off following opposite routes.
His eyes narrowed as he twisted an apple stem
until it broke away cleanly from the fruit.
It must be like the moon and tides, he said.
But I told him even the trickle from the tap
made its decision here, left or right.
Where does the rain turn as it falls
in half, parting like hair, and what happens
to someone who weeps in this zone?
We passed fields of winter cabbages,
a thousand rows twirling out in straight
lines no matter how you eyed them.
And how would these cabbages roll,
he smiled. Uneasy with new facts of science,
he feigned abrupt fatigue and laziness
when it was a matter of sadness.
His eyes no longer followed the zinc edge
of the horizon against that early winter sky.
In a far pasture, I saw two buzzards
circling a darkness on the turf.
A dead calf, I thought.
Whatever it was,
it rose and shook itself.

I watched until the heavy birds
unwound from their spiral
and flew apart.

Maria Flook, 1990

Legacy

In Wheeling, West Virginia, inmates riot.
Two cut out the heart of a child rapist
and hold it steaming in a guard's face
because he will live
                        to tell the story.
They know they have already died
of unrequited love
                        and in another version
won't recognize the murdered
as he walks toward them
                        disguised as the betrayed lover.
I don't know the ending,
or how this will make the bruised and broken
child live easier into the night
                        of a split world,
where in one camp the destroyers
                        have cooked up
a stench of past and maggots.
                        And in the other
love begins a dance, a giveaway to honor
the destroyed with new names.
I don't know the ending.
But I know the legacy of maggots is wings.
And I understand how lovers can destroy everything
                                together.

Joy Harjo, 1990

Song for the Deer and Myself
to Return On

For Louis Oliver

This morning when I looked out the roof window
before dawn and a few stars were still caught
in the fragile weft of ebony night
I was overwhelmed. I sang the song Louis taught me:
a song to call the deer in Creek, when hunting,
and I am certainly hunting something as magic as deer
in this city far from the hammock of my mother's belly.
It works, of course, and deer came into this room
and wondered at finding themselves
in a house near downtown Denver.
Now the deer and I are trying to figure out a song
to get them back, to get all of us back,
because if it works I'm going with them.
And it's too early to call Louis
and nearly too late to go home.

Joy Harjo, 1990

Eagle Poem

To pray you open your whole self
To sky, to earth, to sun, to moon
To one whole voice that is you.
And know there is more
That you can't see, can't hear,
Can't know except in moments
Steadily growing, and in languages
That aren't always sound but other
Circles of motion.
Like eagle that Sunday morning
Over Salt River. Circled in blue sky
In wind, swept our hearts clean
With sacred wings.
We see you, see ourselves and know
That we must take the utmost care
And kindness in all things.

Breathe in, knowing we are made of
All this, and breathe, knowing
We are truly blessed because we
Were born, and die soon within a
True circle of motion,
Like eagle rounding out the morning
Inside us.
We pray that it will be done
In beauty.
In beauty.

Joy Harjo, 1990

from *Articulation of Sound Forms in Time*

from 1. The Falls Fight

Land! Land! Hath been the idol of many in New England!—*Increase Mather*

Just after King Philip's War so-called by the English and shortly before
King William's War or Governor Dudley's War called the War of the
Spanish Succession by Europeans, Deerfield was the northernmost co-
lonial settlement in the Connecticut River Valley. In May 1676 several
large bands of Indians had camped in the vicinity. The settlers felt threat-
ened by this gathering of tribes. They appealed to Boston for soldiers,
and a militia was sent out to drive away Squakeags, Pokomtucks, Mahi-
cans, Nipmunks, and others. The standing forces were led by Captain
Turner of Boston. Captain Holyoke brought a contingent from Spring-
field; Ensign Lyman, a group from Northampton. Sergeants Kellog and
Dickinson led the militia from Hadley. Benjamin Wait and Experience
Hinsdale were pilots.
    "The Reverend Hope Atherton, minister of the gospel, at Hatfield, a
gentleman of publick spirit, accompanied the army."
    The small force of 160 men marched from Hatfield on May 17, shortly
before nightfall. They passed the river at Cheapside where they were
heard by an Indian sentinel who aroused his people. Indians searched the
normal fording place but the colonial militia had missed it by accident.
Finding no footprints they assumed the sentry had been deceived by the
noise of moose passing along the river. The colonial troops continued on
their way until they happened on an unguarded Nipmunk, Squakeag,
Pokomtuck, or Mahican camp. This they immediately attacked by firing
into the wigwams. Wakened from sleep the frightened inhabitants

thought they were being raided by Mohawks. The chronicler writes: "They soon discovered their mistake but being in no position to make an immediate defense were slain on the spot, some in their surprise ran directly to the river, and were drowned; others betook themselves to their bark canoes, and having in their confusion forgot their paddles, were hurried down the falls and dashed against the rocks. In this action the enemy by their own confession, lost 300, women and children included."

What the historian doesn't say is that most of the dead were women and children.

Only one white man was killed at what came to be called *The Falls Fight*. Indian survivors soon rallied neighboring bands and when they realized that the English force was only a small one, they pursued and harassed the victorious retreating army. Now thirty-seven soldiers were killed and several more wounded. The soldiers were retreating because they had run out of ammunition. The retreat soon became a rout. About twenty members of the militia stood their ground and fired at the pursuing Native Americans who were crossing the river. After a hard skirmish they rejoined the body of the now surrounded army, and together they fought their way ten miles back to safety. Except for Hope Atherton and seven or eight others who were somehow separated from their fellows. These Christian soldiers soon found themselves lost. After hiding in the woods for several days some of them came to the Indians and offered to surrender on the condition that their lives would be spared. But the Squakeags, Nipmunks, Pokomtucks, or Mahicans, instead of giving them quarter, covered each man with dry thatch. Then they set the thatch on fire and ordered each soldier to run. When one covering of thatch was burnt off, another was added, and so these colonists continued running, until, Indians later told the historian: "Death delivered them from their hands."

Prophesie is Historie antedated; and History is Postdated Prophesie.

 John Cotton

In our culture Hope is a name we give women. Signifying desire, trust, promise, does her name prophetically engender pacification of the feminine?

Pre-revolution Americans viewed America as the land of Hope.

"The Reverend Hope Atherton, minister of the gospel, at Hatfield, a gentleman of publick spirit, accompanied the army."

Hope's baptism of fire. No one believed the Minister's letter. He became a stranger to his community and died soon after the traumatic exposure that has earned him poor mention in a seldom opened book.

Hope's literal attributes. Effaced background dissolves remotest foreground. Putative author, premodern condition, presently present what future clamors for release?

Hope's epicene name draws its predetermined poem in.

I assume Hope Atherton's excursion for an emblem foreshadowing a Poet's abolished limitations in our demythologized fantasy of Manifest Destiny.

Susan Howe, 1990

from 2. Hope Atherton's Wanderings

Prest try to set after grandmother
revived by and laid down left ly
little distant each other and fro
Saw digression hobbling driftwood
forage two rotted beans & etc.
Redy to faint slaughter story so
Gone and signal through deep water
Mr. Atherton's story Hope Atherton

———

Clog nutmeg abt noon
scraping cano muzzell
foot path sand and so
gravel rubbish vandal
horse flesh ryal tabl
sand enemys flood sun
Danielle Warnare Servt
Turner Falls Fight us
Next wearer April One

———

Soe young mayde in March or April laught
who was lapd M as big as any kerchief
as like tow and beg grew bone and bullet
Stopt when asleep so Steven boy companion
Or errant Socoquis if you love your lives
War closed after Clay Gully hobbling boy

laid no whining trace no footstep clue
"Deep Water" he *must* have crossed over

———

Who was lapt R & soe grew bone & bullet
as like tow and as another scittuation
Stopt when Worshp Steven boy companion
Abt noon and abt sun come Country Farm
Follow me save me thithter this winter
Capt. Turner little horn of powder
Medfield Clay Gully hobbling boy
Sixteen trace no wanton footstep rest
Soe struck fire set the woods on fire

———

Susan Howe, 1990

from 3. Taking the Forest

Corruptible first figure
Bright armies wolves warriors steers

scorned warning captive compulsion

Love leads to edge
Progress of self into illusion

Same and not the same
Cherubim intone their own litany

Universal separation
—Distant coherent rational system

Vault lines divergence
Atom keystone

Parmenides prohibition
End of passageway perceive surrounding

Consciousness grasps its subject
Stumbling phenomenology

infinite miscalculation of history

Great men thicker than their stories
sitting and standing

to mark suns rising and setting
Ridges of sand rising on one another

Mathematics of continua

fathomless infinitesimal fraction
sabbatical safety beyond seven

Empty arms cloud counterfeit

antecedent terror stretched to a whisper

———

Susan Howe, 1990

The Children

The children are hiding among the raspberry canes.
They look big to one another, the garden small.
Already in their mouths this soft fruit
That lasts so briefly in the supermarket
Tastes like the past. The gritty wall,
Behind the veil of leaves, is hollow.
There are yellow wasps inside it. The children know.
They know the wall is hard, although it hums.
They know a lot and will not forget it soon.

When did we forget? But we were never
Children, never found where they were hiding
And hid with them, never followed
The wasp down into its nest
With a fingertip that still tingles.
We lie in bed at night, thinking about

The future, always the future, always forgetting
That it will be the past, hard and hollow,
Veiled and humming, soon enough.

Mark Jarman, 1990

The Black Riviera

For Garrett Hongo

There they are again. It's after dark.
The rain begins its sober comedy,
Slicking down their hair as they wait
Under a pepper tree or eucalyptus,
Larry Dietz, Luis Gonzalez, the Fitzgerald brothers,
And Jarman, hidden from the cop car
Sleeking innocently past. Stoned,
They giggle a little, with money ready
To pay for more, waiting in the rain.

They buy from the black Riviera
That silently appears, as if risen,
The apotheosis of wet asphalt
And smeary-silvery glare
And plush inner untouchability.
A hand takes money and withdraws,
Another extends a sack of plastic—
Short, too dramatic to be questioned.
What they buy is light rolled in a wave.

They send the money off in a long car
A god himself could steal a girl in,
Clothing its metal sheen in the spectrum
Of bars and discos and restaurants.
And they are left, dripping rain
Under their melancholy tree, and see time
Knocked akilter, sort of funny,
But slowing down strangely, too.
So, what do they dream?

They might dream that they are in love
And wake to find they are,

That outside their own pumping arteries,
Which they can cargo with happiness
As they sink in their little bathyspheres,
Somebody else's body pressures theirs
With kisses, like bursts of bloody oxygen,
Until, stunned, they're dragged up,
Drawn from drowning, saved.

In fact, some of us woke up that way.
It has to do with how desire takes shape.
Tapered, encapsulated, engineered
To navigate an illusion of deep water,
Its beauty has the dark roots
Of a girl skipping down a high-school corridor
Selling Seconal from a bag,
Or a black car gliding close to the roadtop,
So insular, so quiet, it enters the earth.

Mark Jarman, 1990

The Gift

When I was five my father kidnapped me.
He didn't keep me long enough to worry
My mother. And I wonder if she knew.
But I knew, five years old. That day at school,
He waited for me at the double doors,
His Hudson parked behind him, ready to go.
I knew he'd come when he was not supposed to.
He said it was all right, my mother knew.
On the front seat, there was a present for me,
And as he started, he said I could unwrap it.
The ribbon wouldn't give, the gift box buckled.
But he was driving, couldn't stop to help.
Outside the windshield traffic lights hung down
From cables, and the bushy tops of palms
Showed up at intervals that I could count.
A pink or yellow building front skimmed past.
But mostly I could only see the sky.
A child could hardly see from those old cars
With the window set up high above your shoulder.

The sky went by, pale blue and white and empty,
Crossed suddenly by wire. And I gave up
Trying to take the wrapping off my present
Until we reached wherever we were going.
Then, at a stop, one of those tall palm trees
That wears a shaggy collar of dead fronds
Leaned down and opened up the door and got in
Beside me. Daddy called her Charlotte dear
and told her I was Susan. Sitting down,
She was the tallest woman, and she wore
A high fur collar with white points of hair.
She let me put my hand on them. So soft!
I was excited then, because she helped me
Unwrap my gift and set me on her lap
So I could see. It was a long drive then,
Through orange groves where all the fruit was green,
Past dairy farms that you could smell right through
The rolled-up windows and even through the sweetness
Of Charlotte's perfume and Daddy's after-shave.
We went down through a canyon to the beach
And Charlotte pointed at a pair of wings,
Two bars of black and white that drifted high
Above the gap. She said it was a condor.
Against the ocean, where the canyon ended,
A roller coaster's highest hump rose up.
Beside it was a dome with colored flags.
By this time in the afternoon, at home,
Mother would listen to the radio
And pretty soon I'd have to go indoors
For dinner. Daddy bought me a corn dog,
An Orange Julius, and, for dessert,
The biggest cotton candy in the world.
But first I rode the carousel three times.
From there, as I pumped slowly up and down,
I had a good look at the two of them—
Daddy, like a blond boulder, round and bald,
And Charlotte, though I knew how soft she was,
Like a palm tree still, looking stiff and spiky.
I knew he loved me (maybe she did, too),
But soon he'd have to take me home to Mother.
Around us broke a bank of evening fog,
Softly but coldly, too. We had to leave.

Later I fell asleep on Charlotte's arm,
Her fox fur floating lightly on my hair
And Daddy's present open on my lap.
I wish I'd kept awake to have my say
That day, that one day clearer than all my childhood.
Next morning I awoke in my own bed,
And Mother asked if I'd had fun with Daddy.
He'd kidnapped me. She didn't seem to know it!
Daddy and Charlotte never married. Mother
Went on as if he were a kindly neighbor
Dropping in now and then to help her with me.
We'll see if that's the way I treat your father.
I can't recall what the gift was he gave me.

Mark Jarman, 1990

Sunrise and Moonfall, Rosarito Beach

What I remember of Mexico
is how the glass apple of mescal glowed
and exploded like a globe of seeds
or something we couldn't pronounce
or know the secret name of, never,
and even when the federales shook us down for twenty bucks
as they must, to save face,
I couldn't lose the curve and rupture
of that sphere—half-full, hand-blown, imperfect
as our planet. Sure, everything is blowing open
now, all the freeways and skinheads, the music
invisibly blasting, radio waves invading the spines and craniums
of all this. San Diego, Tijuana, the Beach of Dead Dogs
where we slept in the cold, local kids incredulous
of Ed up early for no reason
driving golf balls out into the restlessly pounding surf.
Jesus, we're always hitting golf balls. It seems to be
some irreducible trait. There's Rob smashing the plaster icons,
all the bleeding martyrs and aqua pigs
and pink squinting Virgins the radiant chapel of candles
induced us to need. Jesus, let me ask, please,
before he decapitates you also with a wicked six-iron slice,
why are we always the ones on the beach

as dawn sucks the last drops fr
the ones who beat the sacred igua
as the sun comes right up
and the shadow-globe finally dances off
the moon, I mean,
that other white world of men
driving golf balls to seas of dust and oblivion—
chrome-headed, flag-waving, violent, American.

Campbell McGrath, 1990

What They Drank

Water, rarely. Sometimes goat's milk, later cow's. Never coffee or tea:
too expensive to import.
Liquor reigned: flagons of ale, casks and demijohns of fine French brandy,
costly decanters of Spanish port,

all laboriously shipped or smuggled, until at last the miracle grain
of the New World, corn,
was mashed and fermented into whiskey at great pecuniary gain.
Thus was born

our second-oldest industry: distilling. Though the wild Concord grape
   lacked
flavor, breweries spread withal;
the growth of orchards led to cider and applejack,
peach brandy in the South a windfall.

Also popular were mixed drinks: cider & rum, cider & mead,
above all *flip*, being beer
sweetened with molasses or pumpkin, fortified with spirit alcohol as needed,
then scalded with a hot poker.

Lastly came rum from the Indies, called "kill-devil" by the Dutch,
   Manhattan awash
with the diabolical liquor,
said worse even than gin: worse for the poor because cheaper, worse
for the rich because quicker.

Campbell McGrath, 1990

t black,
: was!
ind back,
e-black,
1at was.

1al Film.'' Sure,
: no one to dock it.
h insurance:

ns from the docket!

hite ashes
lide/merge:
:lash
as *ashes.*

Stars, timber, ships, men: all manner of destinies converge.

Campbell McGrath, 1990

Survey

I am so lonely for the twentieth century,
for the deeply felt, obscene graffiti
of armed men and the beautiful bridges
that make them so small and carry them
into the hearts of cities written like words
across nothing, the dense void
history became in my beautiful century.
When a man talks reason, he postpones something.
He gets in the way of a machine that knows him
for the sad vengeance he is, somewhere close
to the bald name of his city. ''New York''
means ''strike back.'' ''Attica'' means ''strike back''
and so does any place in the world
in the huge eyes and tender hands of my century.

I went to the capital. I had a banner
and there were thousands of people like me.

There was an airplane, and for a moment
heavy with laurel and sprays of peach blossom
something that had never happened before
stretched like a woman's shadow on a hedge
between the plane and the people who saw it flying.
It was the real name of the century.
It told everyone to strike back
until there was no reason in the world
except a machine stalled overhead
that knows everyone and is as delicate
as peach blossom. But the poor years come too late.

Donald Revell, 1990

New Dark Ages

The loose stonework and an outdated sense of freedom
like the word "airship" or like the fragmentary
sense memory I have of reading books in a cloister
on my birthday when the sunlight is always pure.
These things slip from the rail of a long terrace.
They fall into the street and past it, into the river.
And inside me, the airship lifts and swells
and people in turn-of-the-century costume
laugh with amazement as the loose stonework
and our lives fall as the airship rises.

I've never had much real control over things.
The music of pianos, for example, is the dead world
where I loved the machine of my small freedoms,
one of the crowd in his best clothes despite the weather,
the Eastern snow like the distinct sound of pianos
over the airfield. The music lifts and swells.
I remember this or that. And then a loose stone falls
and I am alone on the terrace of the longest,
best century, looking into the air for music
where there is none, all of it disappeared—
stonework breaking the surface of a river,
the lyric snow a thousand atoms of silence
skating over the surface. All I've ever done
is to wait, to gasp at the take-off and flight

of what I just barely feel. My freedom
as it was taken away early.
The sunlight stilling a cloister on my birthday.

The air is filled with ships.
A machine plays many pianos at once
and the music holds them aloft, a different tune
for each ship. Freedom has nothing to do with control
and control nothing to do with my weak heart
lonely for its birthday and the excitement
of pure sunlight and of snow parting
into countless buoyant shapes over the airfield.
A long, long century is crumbling around me.
There is much to remember, and I want
to give it all away, to become lighter than air.

Donald Revell, 1990

Muse

You are somewhere very close to the porch.
The evening makes crazy sounds, but makes sense.
The unpackaged, greeny neighborhood settles
into true night far from the expressway
and farther from the calligrams of the downtown.
The visits to the paintings failed me.
The new music faded underground with the last trains,
with stripped hours and many lovers.

I did not imagine a stronger life,
listening for your step on the porch step,
imagining your dress a size too large
billowing the obscene print of summer.
Anything composed is an obscenity:
a painter's phlox in vertical brushstrokes,
a dressmaker's parody of stupid earth,
a radio's jazz clawed by cats.

A stronger life exists but is no one's friend.
She lives in the crook of the expressway
in a high building. She tucks her hair behind

her ears and carries a clear drink to the window.
No one ever paints her portrait. Her name
is ugly and can't be put to music.
And at her neck and ankles a long dress
blackens calligrams I read with my fingers.

The truth of those black messages is cold.
The imagination has no power over life,
and between inspirations that are lovers
and inspirations that are a kind of machinery
repainted every year but irreparable
the only thing actual at day's end
is night's uncomposed, leafy tunelessness.
I will not open the door when you arrive.

I will not call my lost loves to wish them well.
In my house in darkness behind the porch
I pound the walls and make an animal noise
as the neighborhood rises and runs en masse
onto the expressway to be destroyed
or dragged downtown to touch the calligrams
and feel nothing that is green, made, or harmonious.
It is loveless time, the neck and ankles of time.

I need more loneliness than alone is,
the deep, uninspired dark of America
where sexy lawns, the phlox, the print dresses
and hymn stanzas like tiny, circular railroads
ask for no response and no love
but a clear drink in the solitary evening
when no muse visits, when crazy animal sounds
make sense and I read the truth with my hands.

Donald Revell, 1993

Audubon *Enfant*

I First
met the light and shook it
Aux Cayes, my mother la créole Rabin
who dies. I am one. Father finds

for me a stepmother and they
together a half-
sister, Muguet called Rosa,
& he is away. In his fields
I cut pieces of cane for me & Rosa
to suck. I am Jean.
My father *marin* learned
this language in an English prison.
Later I count my days from France sometimes,
this place Saint Domingue *maman* hard
to remember. New

world it is, my warm
island, wilderness churning
beyond the lines of coffee plants. The woman
names me again *Fougère* you would say Fern,
names are charms and we need them.
There are places I cannot take the little one.
Edges of things are dangerous—where
sea and land meet, or field and forest,
things get loose from their names.
On the edge of my family I call myself
LaForêt my first self before I knew
French or african or english words.
I saw red birds sign themselves in air
before they sang, flourishing.
"Parroquet. Trogon." She carried me outdoors
& I reached for them, my stepmother said.
I am Jean Jacques Fougère LaForêt Rabin
Audubon.

Pamela Alexander, 1991

At Coueron. My First Gun.

Mama & I
& Rosa, we hope never to meet
another war. Here
the land is flat & trim, sheep
swerve together, hedges & fences
keep order. I explore

margins & flawed places
while Rosa's piano turns
a pretty flurry. I take chocolate
in waxy papers & a basket
to bring back nests & lichens, more strange
than my lessons. The daily murders of the city are far, fewer,
then stop, & I forget them.

We grow
apart, my sister
and I, she domestic, says
my blown eggs & stuffed birds
stink. I close the door.

I shoot well, corks I toss
come down in showers, my fingers gleam
with powder. The gun kicks my shoulder,
its shout & smell clear me.
The bird falls,
always. I watch its color & shine & flare
for weeks before I fire, but my sketch preserves
only its deadness. I burn
my pencil's generation of cripples
on my birthday.

Sometimes I sleep
near my Originals, on leaf litter
beneath the trees they close their eyes in,
sometimes I lie awake in the quiet house
& listen to the nightwatch
kept by the river, old water clock,
& by whickering horses standing
to their sleep.

Pamela Alexander, 1991

Distances

I love calling west through time zones,
the telephone company's map open before me
with its miniature clocks and the deep fissure

in the middle where the binding is,
my disembodied voice traveling left
past the sprinkling of familiar cities on the East Coast
through the places where weather is harvested
and states grow bigger, their names
more voweled, where the Green Giant
lies staked to the ground,
the weight of his body flattening the Midwest,
the foliage of his hair ripe for shearing,
for the preserving cold of refrigerated trucks.
I love the fact that there is no discernible
elapsed time between exit and entrance,
that my voice circumnavigates the hidden passages
of someone's ear before I pause for breath.
For that listener it is not yet evening,
though beyond my window the outlines of trees blur
as if the onset of night gives them permission
to loosen the boundaries of their thingness
while my voice journeys back in time
to the afternoon where everyone is always
a few hours behind me, more innocent.
And I could be there too; I could fly westward
shedding seconds along the way, arriving
before I phoned, to answer my own call,
that abstraction, and rush my words
forward along the line, to interrupt myself
at the moment my plane crosses overhead
and I look down through layers of cloud light
to seek the intersection of my voices
where self, released from place, at last consists of
the velocity of union it attains.

Claire Bateman, 1991

Another Kimono

So many poems with kimonos
opening darkly. Drifting over us
from the blackest corners
of touch and kiss. Kimonos
our bodies aren't worthy of

until bodies are shed
like a mottled skin that hurts
when we peel it off.
Whichever broken birdcage
my father saw clean through,
Hiroshima or Nagasaki, he
isn't too sure anymore, and you
can't hear even one wave
lap into his voice that sailed
too quietly over the ocean
and home again. You can't hear
what went into the looking
more and more finely
that rubble seldom teaches us
how to stop. How to see
each glint without wondering
what larger brightness it must have
belonged to. Each flame
on the back of the dragon
was larger and sillier
than its red tiny marvelous
angry stitches. So he bought
a black silk robe instead
and brought it home to my mother
along with his sailor hat
and a green mottled box
with a white silk lining
and rows of Japanese characters
like dancers with too many broken
arms and legs. Inside
its foreignness there was
nothing. Did she put the robe
on when they touched,
small flames burning everywhere
to forget the bitter cold
sunny afternoon, did they lie
down together and take off
everything but the bare trees
with bark dull and black
like a shining
turned in on itself?

Nancy Eimers, 1991

No Friends of the Heart

Believing the heart was the center of knowledge,
the ancient Egyptians would leave it inside the mummified body
and hope the other organs, bottled and placed near the catafalque,
might be put to some more enlightened use.
The summer I worked in a factory
I was told by Edelmira to stay in college
to learn more wonderful stories
and teach them to others.
I would say we were almost friends,
working across the table from each other,
oiling and polishing notebook binders and stacking boxes
all day, every day
in a white fluorescent eternity.
By midafternoon the women from Cuba and Puerto Rico and Mexico
had made each other lonely
by talking in Spanish too intimately,
parents, husbands, children, brothers, sisters,
names that went by and imagined the rest,
all the details that get so homesick
we can't stay long with each other's lives.
But when Edelmira was generous with my future,
imagining a white room with windows
and the sound of my voice addressing itself
to a classroom's shy and receptive silences,
she was leaving herself in the dingy present,
the little table with somebody else across from her,
the piles of binders, ring after ring after ring
that would not meet. When I tried to be cheerful—
you have so many friends here—
she answered, putting her hand on her chest,
no friends of the heart.
She said it in English and it sounded true,
breaking out of her language and into mine
with the urgency that has still not learned
to be indirect.
If there is another life,
I hope it is ruled by affection,
which in this life we can only restore to each other
unexpectedly, a chance bit of news, an odor,
an old, bleak feeling just biding its time.

It seems in this life the heart is not yet the center of knowledge,
but we have always been in awe of blood.
When I sat by the pond with you a few days ago
you said one reason to have a child
is so lovers can dwell at last in a single body.
But friends can't live in each other's bodies.
If sometimes language fails them
less than their looking quietly at each other,
if vocalizations, gestures, expressions
are meaningless layers we have to cut through somehow,
I don't know what we will find inside.
For now, all we can do is take care of each other
from the outside,
as when mosquitoes swirled up from the grass
and we brushed them off each other's arms and faces and hair.

Nancy Eimers, 1991

Night Sweats 2

For Michael Canter

Two men lie folded in sleep,

                     a blue sheet draped over their bodies.

One, awakening to the other's sweat,

                     slips out to get the damp cloth they keep

refrigerated for nights like this.

                     If the other wakes, he'll weep and shake.

So the one does the best he can to gentle him

                     through the delirium and back into dream.

Tonight the other tries something different.

                     He holds his breath, releasing the air

so gradually, he finds he can almost keep

the shaking away. He lies so still

in the arms of the one he loves

                that the one who loves him imagines

for an instant as he drifts into sleep

                that the other no longer breathes.

Boyer Rickel, 1991

Poem to Begin the Second Decade of AIDS

The dog, alive, Lucy, my light, sleeps
    on the couch I'd have trained her off of
had not someone coaxed her, repeatedly,
    to clamber up, then lie down along
his outstretched legs; Gary, alive, who,

    had he had his way at first, wouldn't
have let her live with us at all for fear
    she'd dig up the bulbs and seedlings,
or strip the bark from young acacias
    and mesquites in our yard alive with

four years of his ceaseless shovel, shoulder,
    rake and sweat. The hour darkens, sweetens,
whenever I ask how long for all of this—
    November lettuces, April poppies, Lucy's
dog-fragrant, humid *hrumph* across my

    rising/falling, almost-sleeping chest,
how long the *chauk, chauk* of Gary's spade,
    the swells and waves of caliche and dust.
This poem is far too private for anybody
    but us. This poem will make certain

close friends blush, who prefer poems be
    like linens they can put in drawers,
sure of their place and use. Today I

thought of this as I took up our blue
wool blanket, a week-long winter freeze

    having passed, folding once, twice,
a cloudless, geometrically diminishing sky;
    then twice again, all compact, tangible
potential, ready to unfold and warm or
    simply drape across a reclining form.

January 1990

Boyer Rickel, 1991

Chestnuts for Verdi

Roncole, 1984

Loose, drifting in pools
of black water, the gravel slushes
as a pair of peahens crosses
the path, stabbing for seeds.
The one I gather from a tuft of grass
pushing up the stones
is too large for them: a chestnut,
hard and glazed,
like the belly of a mare
or the unbroken shore of a piano
where a singer leans, pressing out
the notes into the morning's stillness.

And he is there, arched
over the yellowed keys, his silhouette
as soft as the fingers cupped
around this fruit. The sunlight
slips between the salon drapes,
and a wagon filled with
oak, birch, and chestnut
enters the scrolled gate.
Each new stump waits
for the gray lip of soil
with a patience only trees have.
While the birds come and go,

like lovers frightened
by their own strange music.

The paths shoot off everywhere—
into the trees, the fields,
and one to the maestro's door where
a woman waits with her coin dish
to take us in. Into a web of rooms
unlit by the morning, into a silence
as false as the flowers
old women leave on his grave.

Yet the chestnuts bulging
out of her pockets are there
for anyone to see. Now they can
bring fire to a man's touch
and they'll do nicely in a pudding.
And the snow-tipped branches
which they left behind
rise and fall like heavy arms
coaxing the air, keeping
the music of the earth
close to the earth.

Roberta Spear, 1991

The Sighting

Maybe half a mile offshore the surface darkening
as if to a gust of wind, then five or six
elongated coils moving in single file
right to left, glistening, clearly *there*, as she
squints into the low afternoon sun, shading her eyes,
feeling her heart rise to the occasion, wondering
if she's actually been singled out and chosen
to see in the next instant a face rising
from the lake's million dents, perhaps that of a dog
with little winglike ears, the face she noticed once
in a granite panorama above the portals
of a French cathedral, the saved going this way,
everyone else going that, but here

and now looking around, its gaze fiery with perception,
scanning the waters, the shoreline farther off
and the bluffs above, not failing to recognize
the human figure there whose very immobility
prompts the impulse to turn toward it and investigate—

while she keeps asking it to pause
in its actual, unresponsive progress, not sure she wants
anything (a sound she's never heard, hoarse clanging
like bells and static?), but willing to settle for
the slightest sign from whatever it is
as it continues leftward, more and more out of her hands,
like yesterday or merely a minute ago, a few recursive glints
in its wake suggesting the presence of a real
unknown creature, but one so involved
in the element of its unconcern that when she looks again
she sees nothing but the lake's final, momentary
smithereens as the sun vanishes, her sighting
already something other than what meets the eye,
restored to those shadowy canyons where green
disappears into the depths of night, the first stars
becoming distinct, and the stillness around her
no longer listening as she closes her eyes
for one more wordless attempt at calling it back.

Jonathan Aaron, 1992

Kinshasa

Every morning the Pope kisses Africa.
The map on his wall has 4 corners,
like the wall.
When he kisses Africa,
it's usually Zaire.

The Pope says "I like how my lower
back feels at that angle
I bend to kiss Zaire.
To kiss Egypt I have to balance
on the tips of my toes."

What the Pope secretly wants to kiss
is only the capital of Zaire,
but his lips are too big for that;
try as he might, he kisses *all* Zaire,
and sometimes a bit of Burundi.

Walid Bitar, 1993

Looking You in the Back of the Head

I'll compare you to the outskirts of Copenhagen,
I'll compare you to a swan made of twisted
coat-hangers, to Mars, to a toad, to pink
gum stretched from the pavement by a clog, to a rose,
a mailman's uniform, the Klondike Goldrush,
popcorn spilled on a black velvet purse,
an alligator, a sky blue bongo drum,
a pomegranate with many cavities, a pine nut,
an unsigned income tax return, I'll compare
you to a pear, an avocado, I don't care
as long as after all is said and done
it wasn't you I was talking about—let all
these comparisons be so much confetti decking out
the cathedral of amnesia which, by the way,
is not a cathedral at all, it's a labyrinth,
a celebration, onion soup, a mallard, and yes
I'm happy the neighbors love us very much
because they're gulls made of swans made of twisted
coat-hangers, and all my clothes are on the floor, and I'm—
naked? No, this is not my body—*you're* naked;
get away from my clothes; I love those clothes!
From now on you do what I do, you are me,
not you at all—I'll do what you like, like plantains,
like apple pie, double digit inflation, and then baboons.
In return, repeat after me: I. Now it's your turn: "I."

Walid Bitar, 1993

Appendix: Wesleyan Poetry

Author	Title	Year	Series
Aaron, Jonathan	*Corridor*	1992	
Akers, Ellery	*Knocking on the Earth*	1989	WNP
Alexander, Pamela	*A Commonwealth of Wings*	1991	
Ali, Agha Shahid	*The Half-Inch Himalayas*	1987	WNP
Alonso, Ricardo	*Cimarron*	1978	WPP 94
Angel, Ralph	*Anxious Latitudes*	1986	WNP
Ansen, Alan	*Disorderly Houses*	1961	WPP 11
Ashbery, John	*The Tennis Court Oath*	1962	WPP 13
Bagg, Robert	*Madonna of the Cello*	1961	WPP 9
Bateman, Claire	*Bicycle Slow Race*	1991	WNP
Baumel, Judith	*The Weight of Numbers*	1988	
Beasley, Bruce	*Spirituals*	1988	WNP
Benedikt, Michael	*The Body*	1968	WPP 40
Benedikt, Michael	*Mole Notes*	1971	WPP
Benedikt, Michael	*Sky*	1970	WPP 52
Benedikt, Michael	*Night Cries*	1976	WPP 80
Berke, Judith	*White Morning*	1989	WNP
Bernstein, Lisa	*The Transparent Body*	1989	WNP
Bishop, Elizabeth	*An Anthology of Twentieth-Century Brazilian Poetry*	1972	WPIT
Bitar, Walid	*2 Guys on Holy Land*	1993	
Bly, Robert	*Silence in the Snowy Fields*	1962	WPP 15
Bogen, Don	*After the Splendid Display*	1986	WNP
Boruch, Marianne	*View from the Gazebo*	1985	WNP
Boruch, Marianne	*Descendant*	1989	
Brasil, Emanuel & Smith, William Jay	*Brazilian Poetry (1950–1980)*	1983	WPIT
Brennan, Karen	*Here on Earth*	1988	WNP
Broumas, Olga	*Black Holes, Black Stockings*	1985	
Bryan, Sharon	*Salt Air*	1983	WNP
Bryan, Sharon	*Objects of Affection*	1987	

WNP: Wesleyan New Poets; WPP: Wesleyan Poetry Program; WPIT: Wesleyan Poets in Translation

Author	Title	Year	Series
Budenz, Julia	From the Gardens of Flora Baum	1984	WNP
Buell, Frederick	Full Summer	1979	WPP 95
Burr, Gray	A Choice of Attitudes	1969	WPP 44
Cardenal, Ernesto	With Walker in Nicaragua	1984	WPIT
Cassity, Turner	Watchboy, What of the Night?	1966	WPP 31
Chigounis, Evan	Secret Lives	1972	WPP 60
Chipasula, Frank Mkalawile	When My Brothers Came Home	1985	
Clipman, William	Dog Light	1981	WPP 102
Collier, Michael	The Clasp and Other Poems	1986	WNP
Collier, Michael	The Folded Heart	1989	
Combs, Tram	saint thomas, poems	1965	WPP 25
Davie, Donald	New and Selected Poems	1961	WPP 12
Davie, Donald	Events and Wisdoms	1965	WPP 27
Davis, Glover	Legend	1988	
Davis, Thulani	Playing the Changes	1985	
Dickey, James	Drowning With Others	1962	WPP 14
Dickey, James	Helmets	1964	WPP 21
Dickey, James	Buckdancer's Choice	1965	WPP 28
Dickey, James	The Central Motion	1983	
Dickey, James	The Whole Motion	1992	
Dickey, William	More Under Saturn	1971	WPP 58
Dimitrova, Blaga	Because the Sea is Black: Poems of Blaga Dimitrova	1989	WPIT
Edson, Russell	The Clam Theater	1973	WPP 64
Edson, Russell	The Reason Why the Closet-Man Is Never Sad	1977	WPP 84
Edson, Russell	Wounded Breakfast	1985	
Eimers, Nancy	Destroying Angel	1991	WNP
Enright, D. J.	The Terrible Shears	1974	WPP 73
Farnsworth, Robert	Three or Four Hills and a Cloud	1982	WPP 106
Farnsworth, Robert	Honest Water	1989	
Ferry, David	On the Way to the Island	1960	WPP 7
Flook, Maria	Sea Room	1990	
Forbes, Calvin	Blue Monday	1974	WPP 70
Francis, Robert	The Orb Weaver	1960	WPP 5
Fuertes, Gloria	Off the Map: Selected Poems	1984	WPIT

Author	Title	Year	Series
Genser, Cynthia	Taking on the Local Color	1977	WPP 85
Gilman, Dugan	Upstate	1971	WPP 55
Glaser, Elton	Relics	1984	WNP
Gordett, Marea	Freeze Tag	1984	WNP
Greenberg, Barbara L.	The Spoils of August	1974	WPP 71
Hadas, Rachel	Slow Transparency	1983	
Hadas, Rachel	A Son from Sleep	1987	
Haines, John	Winter News	1966	WPP 29
Haines, John	The Stone Harp	1971	WPP 56
Haines, John	Cicada	1977	WPP 86
Haines, John	News from the Glacier	1982	
Hall, James Baker	Stopping on the Edge to Wave	1988	
Halperin, Mark	The Measure of Islands	1990	
Hanson, Kenneth	The Uncorrected World	1973	WPP 67
Harjo, Joy	In Mad Love and War	1990	
Harmon, William	Treasury Holiday	1970	WPP 53
Harmon, William	Legion: Civic Choruses	1973	WPP 65
Harmon, William	Mutatis Mutandis: 27 Invoices	1985	
Hemschemeyer, Judith	I Remember the Room Was Filled with Light	1973	WPP 66
Hemschemeyer, Judith	Very Close and Very Slow	1975	WPP 76
Hillman, Brenda	White Dress	1985	WNP
Hillman, Brenda	Fortress	1989	
Hillman, Brenda	Death Tractates	1992	
Hillman, Brenda	Bright Existence	1993	
Hinrichsen, Dennis	The Attraction of Heavenly Bodies	1983	WNP
Hirshfield, Jane	Of Gravity and Angels	1988	
Holan, Vladimir	Mirroring: Selected Poems	1985	WPIT
Hongo, Garrett Kaoru	Yellow Light	1982	WPP 104
Honig, Edwin	Spring Journal: Poems	1968	WPP 41
Howard, Richard	Quantities	1962	WPP 16
Howard, Richard	The Damages	1967	WPP 35
Howard, Richard	Quantities/Damages: Early Poems	1984	WPP
Howe, Susan	Singularities	1990	
Howes, Barbara	Light and Dark	1959	WPP 1

Author	Title	Year	Series
Howes, Barbara	*The Blue Garden*	1972	WPP 62
Howes, Barbara	*Private Signal*	1977	
Hussey, Anne	*Baddeck and Other Poems*	1978	WPP 92
Ignatow, David	*Say Pardon*	1961	WPP 10
Ignatow, David	*Figures of the Human*	1964	WPP 23
Ignatow, David	*Rescue the Dead*	1968	WPP 37
Ignatow, David	*Selected Poems*	1975	
Ignatow, David	*Poems, 1934–1969*	1979	
Ignatow, David	*New and Collected Poems, 1970–1985*	1986	
Ignatow, David	*Shadowing the Ground*	1991	
Irwin, Mark	*Against the Meanwhile*	1988	
Jabès, Edmond	*The Book of Dialogue*	1988	WPIT
Jarman, Mark	*The Black Riviera*	1990	
Justice, Donald	*The Summer Anniversaries*	1960	WPP 6
Justice, Donald	*Night Light*	1967	WPP 33
Kallman, Chester	*Absent and Present*	1963	WPP 17
Karr, Mary	*Abacus*	1987	
Katrovas, Richard	*Green Dragons*	1983	WNP
Katrovas, Richard	*Snug Harbor: Poems*	1986	
Katrovas, Richard	*Public Mirror*	1990	
Kearney, Lawrence	*Kingdom Come*	1980	WPP 98
Kelly, Dave	*Instructions for Viewing a Solar Eclipse*	1972	WPP 61
Komunyakaa, Yusef	*Copacetic*	1984	WNP
Komunyakaa, Yusef	*I Apologize for the Eyes in My Head*	1986	
Komunyakaa, Yusef	*Dien Cai Dau*	1988	
Komunyakaa, Yusef	*Magic City*	1992	
Komunyakaa, Yusef	*Neon Vernacular: New and Selected Poems*	1993	
Lalic, Ivan V.	*Roll Call of Mirrors*	1988	WPIT
LeFevre, Adam	*Everything All at Once*	1978	WPP 89
Lerman, Eleanor	*Armed Love*	1973	WPP 68
Levendosky, Charles	*Perimeters*	1970	WPP 49
Levine, Philip	*Not This Pig*	1968	WPP 38
Li Po and Tu Fu	*Bright Moon, Perching Bird*	1987	WPIT
Lipsitz, Lou	*Cold Water*	1967	WPP 34
Lowery, Mike	*Masks of the Dreamer*	1979	WPP 96

Author	Title	Year	Series
Luhrmann, Thomas	The Objects in the Garden	1982	WPP 107
Machado, Antonio	Times Alone	1983	WPIT
Major, Clarence	Swallow the Lake	1970	WPP 54
McAllester, David P.	Hogans	1987	WPIT
McElroy, Colleen J.	Queen of the Ebony Isles	1984	
McElroy, Colleen J.	Bone Flames: Poems	1987	
McElroy, Colleen J.	What Madness Brought Me Here	1990	
McGrath, Campbell	Capitalism	1990	WNP
McHugh, Heather	To the Quick	1987	
McHugh, Heather	Shades	1988	
McMahon, Lynne	Faith	1988	WNP
McNamara, Robert	Second Messengers	1990	WNP
Mezey, Robert	Evening Wind: Poems	1987	
Miles, Josephine	Kinds of Affection	1967	WPP 36
Miller, Jane	Black Holes, Black Stockings	1985	
Miller, Vassar	Wage War on Silence	1960	WPP 8
Miller, Vassar	My Bones Being Wiser	1963	WPP 19
Miller, Vassar	Onions and Roses	1968	WPP 42
Mitchell, Susan	The Water Inside the Water	1983	WNP
Molloy-Olund, Barbara	In Favor of Lightning	1987	WNP
Morgan, Robert	At the Edge of the Orchard County	1987	
Morgan, Robert	Sigodlin: Poems	1990	
Morgan, Robert	Green River	1991	
Moses, W. R.	Identities	1965	WPP 26
Moses, W. R.	Passage	1976	WPP 81
Mulhern, Maureen	Parallax	1986	WNP
Murray, Joan	Same Water	1990	WNP
Nathan, Leonard	The Day the Perfect Speakers Left	1969	WPP 45
Nolan, James	Why I Live in the Forest	1974	WPP 74
Nolan, James	What Moves Is Not the Wind	1979	WPP 99
Orlen, Steve	Permission to Speak	1978	WPP 90
Orr, Gregory	We Must Make a Kingdom of It	1986	
Orr, Gregory	New and Selected Poems	1988	
Osbey, Brenda Marie	In These Houses	1988	
Petersen, Donald	The Spectral Boy	1964	WPP 22
Piercy, Marge	Breaking Camp	1968	WPP 39

Author	Title	Year	Series
Piercy, Marge	Hard Loving	1969	WPP 46
Pijewski, John	Dinner With Uncle Jozef	1982	WPP 105
Plutzik, Hyam	Apples from Shinar	1959	WPP 2
Prado, Adelia	Alphabet in the Park	1990	WPIT
Raboni, Giovanni	The Coldest Year of Grace	1985	WPIT
Radauskas, Henrikas	Chimeras in the Tower	1986	WPIT
Ramke, Bin	The Erotic Light of Gardens	1989	
Ray, David	Gathering Firewood	1974	WPP 75
Ray, David	Sam's Book	1987	
Ray, David	The Maharani's New Wall and Other Poems	1989	
Revell, Donald	New Dark Ages	1990	
Revell, Donald	Erasures	1992	
Richardson, James	Second Guesses	1984	
Rickel, Boyer	arreboles	1991	WNP
Rilke, Ranier Maria	Sonnets to Orpheus	1987	WPIT
Rogers, Pattiann	The Tattooed Lady in the Garden	1986	
Rogers, Pattiann	Splitting and Binding	1989	
Rollings, Alane	In Your Own Sweet Time	1989	
Rutsala, Vern	The Window	1964	WPP 24
Rutsala, Vern	Paragraphs	1978	WPP 91
Santos, Sherod	The Southern Reaches	1989	
Schwartz, Lloyd	These People	1981	WPP 103
Seay, James	Let Not Your Hart	1970	WPP 50
Seay, James	Water Tables	1974	WPP 72
Sells, Michael A.	Desert Tracings: Six Classic Arabian Odes	1989	WPIT
Shapiro, Harvey	Battle Report	1966	WPP 32
Shapiro, Harvey	This World	1971	WPP 57
Shapiro, Harvey	The Light Holds	1984	
Shapiro, Harvey	National Cold Storage Company: New and Selected Poems	1988	
Shapiro, Norman	Fables from Old French	1982	WPIT
Shaw, Robert	Comforting the Wilderness	1977	WPP 87
Silkin, Jon	Poems, New and Selected	1966	WPP 30
Silkin, Jon	Amana Grass	1971	WPP 59
Simpson, Louis	A Dream of Governors	1959	WPP 3
Simpson, Louis	At the End of the Open Road	1963	WPP 20

Author	Title	Year	Series
Skinner, Jeffrey	*Late Stars*	1985	WNP
Smith, Jordan	*Lucky Seven*	1988	
Spaulding, John	*Walking in Stone*	1989	WNP
Spear, Roberta	*The Pilgrim Among Us*	1991	
Spires, Elizabeth	*Globe*	1981	WPP 101
Stevenson, Anne	*Reversals*	1969	WPP 47
Stringer, A. E.	*Channel Markers*	1987	WNP
Sylvester, Janet	*That Mulberry Wine*	1985	WNP
Tapscott, Stephen	*Mesopotamia*	1975	WPP 78
Tate, James	*Viper Jazz*	1976	WPP 82
Tate, James	*Reckoner: Poems*	1986	
Tate, James	*Distance from Loved Ones*	1990	
Tate, James	*Selected Poems*	1991	
Teillier, Jorge	*From the Country of Nevermore*	1990	WPIT
Tichy, Susan	*A Smell of Burning Starts the Day*	1988	
Tillinghast, Richard	*Sleep Watch*	1969	WPP 48
Tillinghast, Richard	*The Knife and Other Poems*	1980	WPP 100
Tillinghast, Richard	*Our Flag Was Still There*	1984	
Turner, Frederick	*Between Two Lives*	1972	WPP 63
Voigt, Ellen Bryant	*Claiming Kin*	1976	WPP 83
Williams, Sherley	*The Peacock Poems*	1975	WPP 79
Witte, John	*Loving the Days*	1978	WPP 93
Wright, Charles	*The Grave of the Right Hand*	1970	WPP 51
Wright, Charles	*Hard Freight*	1973	WPP 69
Wright, Charles	*Bloodlines*	1975	WPP 77
Wright, Charles	*China Trace*	1977	WPP 88
Wright, Charles	*Country Music: Selected Early Poems*	1982	
Wright, James	*Saint Judas*	1959	WPP 4
Wright, James	*The Branch Will Not Break*	1963	WPP 18
Wright, James	*Shall We Gather at the River*	1968	WPP 43
Wright, James	*Collected Poems*	1972	
Wright, James	*Above the River*	1990	
Young, David	*Foraging: Poems*	1986	
Young, David	*Earthshine*	1988	
Young, David	*Planet on the Desk*	1991	
Young, Dean	*Design with X*	1988	WNP

Author	Title	Year	Series
Young, Dean	*Beloved Infidel*	1992	
Zolynas, Al	*The New Physics*	1979	WPP 97
Zweig, Paul	*Eternity's Woods*	1985	
Zweig, Paul	*Selected and Last Poems*	1989	

Copyrights

Author Index

University Press of New England publishes books under its own imprint and is the publisher for Brandeis University Press, Brown University Press, University of Connecticut, Dartmouth College, Middlebury College Press, University of New Hampshire, University of Rhode Island, Tufts University, University of Vermont, and Wesleyan University Press.

About the Author Michael Collier is Director of the Creative Writing Program at the University of Maryland, College Park, and author of two Wesleyan collections: *The Folded Heart* (1989) and *The Clasp and Other Poems* (1986).

Library of Congress Cataloging-in-Publication Data

The Wesleyan tradition : four decades of American poetry / Michael
    Collier, editor.
        p.   cm. — (Wesleyan poetry)
    ISBN 0–8195–2210–4.
        1. American poetry—20th century.   I. Collier, Michael, 1953–   .   II. Series.
    PS613.W47   1993
    811'.5408—dc20
                                                            93–17846

Design by Sally Harris/Summer Hill Books